AF323827

Criminal Justice
Recent Scholarship

Edited by
Nicholas P. Lovrich

A Series from LFB Scholarly

White Collar Crime in the Mutual Fund Industry

Andrew Peterson

LFB Scholarly Publishing LLC
El Paso 2012

Library of Congress Cataloging-in-Publication Data

Peterson, Andrew, 1978-
  White collar crime in the mutual fund industry / Andrew Peterson.
    p. cm.
  Includes bibliographical references and index.
  ISBN 978-1-59332-516-9 (hardcover : alk. paper)
  1. Mutual funds--Corrupt practices--New York (State) 2. Securities
fraud--New York (State) 3. White collar crimes--New York (State) I.
Title.
  HG4930.P48 2012
  364.16'8--dc23
                                        2012017593

ISBN 978-1-59332-516-9

Printed on acid-free 250-year-life paper.

Manufactured in the United States of America.

Table of Contents

Preface

Mutual funds have enjoyed a reputation as a "safe investment" with low risks. Unlike the rest of the securities industry, they have been relatively free of any scandals or criminal investigations. The mutual fund industry has also seen tremendous growth over the past twenty-five years, as the introduction of retirement accounts turned mutual funds into a staple for investors with an eye toward the future. These factors created a $7 trillion dollar industry with approximately 91 million investors (Swensen, 2005, p. 209). This safe, investment staple was threatened in October 2002, when a hedge fund employee alerted former New York State Attorney General Eliot Spitzer that her fellow employees were late trading and market timing mutual funds; practices which harm long-term investors by skimming a fund's profits. The resulting investigations discovered brokerage firms and mutual fund companies regularly colluding with hedge funds and other large investors to allow these groups to skim almost $5.5 billion per year. Subsequent prosecutions resulted in dozens of cases and over $4 billion in fines and disgorgement (see Appendix 3).

This monograph will provide insight into the series of events known as the late trading and market timing scandal. The goal is to provide an understanding of the cause of the scandal and its effects on investors, but also the regulatory response and reformation process. This is done by using facts and statements about the scandal, as well as criminological, sociological, and economic theories to make sense of the outcomes. In order to accomplish this, I will provide the background and context of the mutual fund industry. Next, I will break the scandal down into three parts: its root causes, regulatory responses by the various actors, and attempts at reform and regulation. This study will result in four primary chapters and a conclusion: the introduction and literature review, an aggregate examination of market timing and late trading cases, the New York Attorney General's response to the scandal, and the SEC and NASD/FINRA's response to the scandal. The first chapter will lay out the history and facts of the mutual fund industry, demonstrating why it is important to America's economy and providing the reader with a basic understanding of its functioning. The second chapter focuses on market timing and late trading cases and identifies themes and typologies that emerge from the numerous cases. This chapter also looks at trends among punishments issued and how these vary depending upon the regulatory body. The third chapter discusses the role of the New York Attorney General's office in both prosecuting and publicizing this scandal. Ultimately, the goal of this chapter will be to answer whether this scandal would have even been discovered without Eliot Spitzer being there at that time. The fourth chapter looks at the traditional financial industry regulators and the role they play in first, allowing these actions to perpetuate and then trying to penalize the actors. Finally, the conclusion will revisit important lessons learned from the previous chapters and analyze how, if at all, the financial and regulatory landscapes have changed since the scandal. This work is important not just in its attempts to improve upon existing criminological, sociological, and economic theory, but also because financial scandals affect everyone and preventing them creates a more stable future.

This book should help advance our understanding of not only the mutual fund scandal, but financial scandals and white-collar crime as a whole. This work is important not just in its attempts to improve upon existing criminological, sociological, and economic theory, but also because financial scandals affect all of us and preventing them can help create a more stable future.

CHAPTER 1

Mutual Funds, Their History, and This Scandal

A mutual fund company is an investment company that pools money from clients to invest in stocks and other securities chosen by a fund manager, or group of managers, to create a portfolio. Each fund company may contain many mutual funds. When an investor buys shares of a mutual fund they are actually purchasing a varied group of securities that diversifies their investments and reduces their risk. This is different from buying shares of a stock, which ties the investor's money to the fortunes of one company. If investors were to purchase all of those investment securities individually, they would pay commissions on each transaction. With a mutual fund, the investor only pays either a transaction fee or a percentage of the gross transaction at the point of purchase or point of sale. Depending on the particular fund, they may even pay a combination of the two fees.

Since a mutual fund is a financial instrument that comprises a collection of stocks, bonds, or other investments, it is priced differently than individual stocks. Mutual funds are priced only once, at the end of each trading day, rather than in real-time, as each individual fund investment could vary second-by-second causing the mutual fund price to change a great deal from one moment to the next. At the close of the market, when the securities have stopped trading, the fund's price is calculated using the closing price of the individual securities that comprise the portfolio. The closing prices are combined and averaged, based upon each security's ratio to the overall fund portfolio. The net from the purchases and sales of the mutual fund is also figured into the mutual fund's value. This determines the price of the mutual fund at the end of that day. This price is set just after 4pm EST (Potts, 1972, pp. 141-142).

The etiology of mutual funds has been as a long-term, "buy and hold" investment. Short-term investments in mutual funds hurt long-term investors because they skim profits from the mutual fund. When a mutual fund manager invests, they place percentages of investors' assets in different securities and a certain amount is kept in cash. The amount of cash kept in a fund eliminates the risk of losing the whole portfolio's value due to market volatility. Cash can also be used to pay those investors who sell their shares. When investors rapidly trade in and out of a fund, more cash is withdrawn to pay them. Also, the increased number of transactions results in more commissions paid by the fund as it buys and sells securities to accommodate its varying pool of monies. These costs either come directly out of the fund's profits or they are passed along to the investor in the form of fees (*Wall Street Journal*, 1999, pp. 104-105). In addition, these transactions may come at times when fund manager has to make transactions at a loss on the investment, further hurting the fund's potential performance.

A Brief History of Mutual Funds

A rudimentary form of a mutual fund, known as an investment fund, began in Switzerland in 1849, when people formed the Société Civile Genèvoise d'Emploi de Fonds (Genovese Civil Society Worker's Funds), a formal system of pooling money together for investment purposes. Although some scholars believe these organizations actually began seventy-five years earlier in the Netherlands with a Dutch Merchant, A. Van Ketwich, who invited investors to form an investment trust named *Eendragt Maakt Magt* (Unity Creates Strength) (Simanauskas & Kucko, 2004, p. 2). Regardless, the definition of investment funds comes from the United Kingdom, where the Foreign & Colonial Company established their "Foreign and Colonial Government Trust" in 1868. They defined the trusts as: "Vehicles which provide the investor of moderate means with the same advantage as large capitalists in diminishing risk in foreign and colonial stock by spreading the investment over a number of stocks" (Russell, 2007, pp. 6-7). These early investment trusts created the basis for the "modern" mutual fund.

The Mutual Fund Industry in the U.S.

The first modern mutual fund began in 1924 when the Massachusetts Investment Trust created a fund open to outside investors. The fund started with approximately two hundred investors and $50,000 in assets. The company also created the original mutual fund structure, a business trust with its own trustees and staff, with a separate firm to distribute their shares through stockbrokers. Mutual fund expert and pioneer John Bogle termed this the "alpha structure". He notes that most funds have evolved into an "omega structure", which he believes contains conflicts of interest that can harm investors. The omega structure has fund families controlled by an external management company that is also responsible to their own shareholders. This management company operates the fund, distributes the shares, supervises and directs the investment portfolio, and usually supplies the fund's officers (Bogle, 2005, pp. 172-173). The conflict comes from fund officers who represent the interests of fund investors, but are also employees of the management company that profits from fees paid by those investors.

After the stock market crash in 1929, the securities industry as a whole underwent numerous changes, including creation of the Securities and Exchange Commission (SEC) to oversee the industry. The Investment Company Act of 1940 created regulation of the mutual fund industry by requiring all funds to register with the SEC and meet standards of operation, disclosure, and securities transactions, such as eliminating the large commissions that distributors charged for mutual funds (Russell, 2007, pp. 46-47). The one major rule the Investment Company Act of 1940 did not include was that of "forward pricing". Under the Investment Company Act of 1940, "backward pricing", which allowed investors to make trades at the previous day's price, was still employed. This pricing loophole was corrected in 1968 when Rule 22c-1 was adopted by the SEC, making forward pricing the standard (Swensen, 2005, pp. 283-285). Forward pricing requires that mutual fund trades be conducted at the next calculated price. The SEC is also in charge of overseeing compliance with these regulations, even though the mutual funds are organized like corporations, under State laws.

When individual retirement accounts (IRAs) were developed in 1981, the mutual funds benefited from those individuals seeking long-term investments with lower risks. Now, mutual funds are also commonly purchased in 401k and other employee retirement accounts.

In 2003, mutual funds comprised almost a quarter, or approximately $3 trillion dollars, of the American retirement asset market. Retirement accounts also accounted for 36.4% of mutual fund assets (Swensen, 2005, p. 210). The mutual fund's popularity as a retirement account investment may come from the shared objectives of long-term investment. Their diversified risk allows the investor more security for retirement, while simultaneously allowing for greater growth potential than other lower risk options.

When the Investment Company Act of 1940 was passed, there were sixty-eight mutual fund companies and approximately $450 million from almost 300,000 investors (Potts, 1972, p. 133). Currently, there is over $7 trillion invested in mutual funds. In 2003, 91 million individuals in 53 million households owned mutual funds. This represented almost half of the households in the United States, and is illustrates 200% growth since 1990 and over 800% growth since 1980 (Swensen, 2005, p. 209).

One of the positive attributes of the mutual fund industry has been a virtual lack of a large scandal, since the Investment Company Act was passed almost 70 years ago. The industry recognizes their relatively clean record, reflected in the statements of former SEC commissioner Harvey Goldschmidt in 2003, "The mutual fund industry has been blessed--and blessed is the only word--by being relatively free of scandal" (Bogle, 2005, p. 142). By the end of 2003, endemic late trading and market timing for preferred clients sullied the industry's former "clean record". This initial investigation into late trading and market timing led to accusations of illegal kickbacks and compensation schemes, excessive fees, and illegal sales of mutual fund class B and class C shares. Those involved in the scandal read like a who's who of American finance: Bank of America, Bank One, Deutsche Bank, Bear Sterns, Merril Lynch, Smith Barney, Charles Schwab, Edward Jones, Janus, Fidelity, Putnam, and Strong Funds, had all engaged in some degree of illegal mutual fund trading.

Discovery of the Scandal

In October of 2002, it was Noreen Harrington-a former executive with the investment arm of the Stern family fortune, which included the Canary Capital Partners hedge fund-who alerted former New York Attorney General Eliot Spitzer's office about her fellow employees' late trading and market timing. Some mutual fund companies were even facilitating these illegal practices. In exchange for permission to trade illegally, hedge funds like Canary Capital gave large amounts of capital to the mutual funds, which increased the mutual fund managers' pay. By the summer of the following year, the Attorney General's office had issued subpoenas for Canary Capital Partners, and Eliot Spitzer began a broader investigation into the mutual fund industry.

The story of illegal and unethical trading practices for mutual funds began well before 2002. In the 1980's Gil Blake developed an investment strategy based on market timing mutual funds, by identifying short-term patterns in their gains, and trading based upon the signals that he had identified. After averaging 40% returns, he began investing for friends-much like a hedge fund (Elkind, 4/19/04). Blake continued this strategy and he became part of a small contingent of investors that practiced market timing in mutual funds, estimated to be between 50-100 individuals. He was conscious of the damage that a market timer could do to a mutual fund, and he approved his activities with each fund prior to investing. He also regulated the number of trades he made to conform to mutual fund rules, and limited the amount of money invested in each fund, so that his trades would not negatively affect the fund's performance (Schwager, 1992, pp. 235-242).

During the early 1990's Blake was profiled in a book in which he detailed his timing strategies. This book, *The New Market Wizards*, popularized Blake's strategy and Blake became inundated with letters and phone calls from potential clients asking him to manage their money. Among that group of investors was Eddie Stern, one of the heirs to the Hartz pet-supply fortune and future manager of Canary Capital Partners. After "The New Market Wizards", Stern teamed up with his brother-in-law Robert Simpson and they invested in a hedge fund that specialized in market timing mutual funds (Schwager, 1992, pp. 235-242). The hedge fund owner eventually got out of the business, but Simpson and Stern continued to market time on their own. The partners were not compliant with the mutual funds' rules on market timing, nor did they limit the dollar amount of their investments to minimize harm to the funds.

During the late 1990's, mutual fund companies realized how prevalent market timing was becoming, and how these acts negatively affected returns for the funds' long-term shareholders. Estimates suggest that market timers cost long-term shareholders over $4 billion per year since 1998-99, when market timing was at its peak (Zitzewitz, 2003). As was discovered in some cases, mutual funds had asked brokerage firms and traders to cease and desist market timing in their funds. In response, traders attempted to disguise their market timing by changing account names and splitting large trades into several smaller trades to avoid detection. Recovered emails from the case against Prudential show that Franklin Templeton and other mutual fund companies had tried to shut off all trading from Prudential's market timing brokers (Thomas Jr., 8/29/06). Stern began to arrange deals with the mutual funds in which he would leave a certain amount of money invested in the fund to boost the assets under the fund's management-directly increasing the fund manager's compensation. In exchange, the mutual fund allowed Stern to market time with a smaller account. Stern eventually stopped the partnership with Simpson and began trading on his own.

In 1999 Stern began to get away from the family business and immersed himself completely in fund timing. It was at this time that Stern formed Canary Capital Partners and began market timing, short-selling mutual funds[1], and late trading, through the brokerage firms that placed mutual fund orders and the third party firms that processed the orders (Elkind, 4/19/04, p. 113-115). The illegal nature of Canary Capital's trading strategies required that Stern and his employees actively recruit new firms that would allow the hedge fund to engage in these practices. This did not prove to be much of an obstacle as Stern quickly created alliances with PBHG, Strong Capital, PIMCO, Invesco, and Alliance. From the summer of 1999 until the end of 2002, Stern's company continued to grow and more mutual fund companies and brokerage firms joined the illegal trading schemes.

The New York Attorney General's office investigation was initially led by David Brown, who was in charge of the state's Investor Protection Bureau. During the course of the investigation, Mr. Brown uncovered two former employees of Canary Capital Partners, James Nesfield and Andrew Goodwin, who gave insight into the illegal late trading and market timing agreements between mutual fund companies and Canary Capital Partners (Sender, et al., 9/09/03). The cooperation from Harrington, Nesfield, and Goodwin created the case against Canary Capital Partners and Eddie Stern. Stern quickly reached a settlement with the New York Attorney General's office and become their star witness, detailing the scope of the scandal and the different players involved (Elkind, 4/19/04, p. 126). The National Association of Securities Dealers (NASD) and the Securities & Exchange Commission (SEC) launched their own investigation into the mutual fund industry, and joined forces with Spitzer and other state Attorney Generals to resolve the cases. The NASD investigated approximately 160 broker-dealers, and thirty of those firms were referred to the department's enforcement division (Dale, 11/26/03, D9). The joint investigation led to dozens of settlements, mutual fund executives and traders being fired and banned from the securities industry, rule changes from the regulatory agencies, a few prison sentences, and over $4.3 billion in fines and disgorgement.

Late Trading and Market Timing

The integrity of a mutual fund's forward pricing system is supposed to be guaranteed through the time-stamping of order tickets as the orders are received by the brokerage firms. Orders are then passed along to a third-party to be processed. It is common for those orders placed near the close of the trading day to be processed well after the market close. This means many orders placed before the 4pm deadline are not actually completed until hours after the deadline has passed. The system is violated when certain customers are allowed to bypass the time-stamping process and place orders after the close of the market, buying or selling their mutual funds at the already determined price. The other manner of late trading involves a brokerage firm colluding with certain privileged investors to place legitimate mutual fund orders when information that is expected to affect the mutual fund's price will be released after the market's close. The order is only processed if the information would benefit the investor. If the information does not benefit the investor, the order is canceled (see Appendix 1). Some late traders in this scandal were allowed to trade up until 9pm EST, taking advantage of earnings or other company news that is traditionally released soon after the market close, and is not reflected until the next price calculation. Eliot Spitzer characterized these practices as "betting on the horse race, after the race has been run." It evokes common themes from financial fraud: elimination of investment risk, victimization of all investors because of preferential treatment given to a privileged few, and destruction of the integrity and trust in the financial markets.

The practice of late trading is illegal and has been outlawed by the Federal Investment Act of 1940 and the Martin Act – a New York State securities law created in 1921 and commonly used to prosecute bogus stock sales and boiler room establishments (McTamaney, 2003). Late trading is unique to mutual funds because they are priced only at the close of the market and have the forward pricing policy.

Despite its prohibition, late trading has been prevalent in the industry. A sample of mutual funds found evidence of late trading in 39 of 66 mutual fund families. If this rate is consistent in the rest of the mutual fund industry, it is estimated that late trading would lead to approximately $400 million in losses for the other investors (Zitzewitz, 2006).

Historically, late trading has been easy for mutual fund insiders. Prior to the passage of the Investment Company Act of 1940, a fund's price would be set at 4pm EST, but that price would not become effective until 10am the following day. This created approximately one hour where the mutual fund was simultaneously trading at two different prices. A riskless arbitrage opportunity was created where investors could simply buy at the low price and sell at the high price, diluting profits of long-term investors. In order to instill investor faith in mutual funds, the Investment Company Act of 1940 mandated that the mutual fund price become effective at the 4pm close. Despite the regulation, the majority of mutual funds still employed backward pricing (Ciccotello et al., 2002, pp. 12-14). Backward pricing created arbitrage opportunities by allowing an investor to buy at the known price while watching the stock market move in their favor. These arbitrage opportunities continued until 1968, when the SEC became concerned about mutual fund arbitrage and adopted rule 22c-1, which instituted "forward pricing" and eliminated the pricing loophole (Securities Exchange Commission [SEC], 1992). As Zitzewitz (2003) notes, "Both the pre-1940 and the pre-1968 arbitrage opportunities reportedly led to substantial dilution of long-term shareholders, and in both cases, action by Congress or the SEC was required before the opportunities were eliminated (Zitzewitz, 2003, p. 7).

Late trading alone did not guarantee a "sure thing". A mutual fund is traditionally a long-term investment and the advantage given by late trading only exists in the short-term. If an investor is able to late trade after hearing good news about a company or sector, and then sell the mutual fund the next day, that person would almost certainly profit. This type of rapid in-out trading is known as market timing and even though it is often committed alone, it has been associated with late trading during this scandal.

While the SEC does not expressly outlaw market timing, it is considered an unethical practice. In addition, each mutual fund prospectus states that the fund does not allow market timing. By allowing market timing, a fund is misrepresenting its position on this harmful practice and defrauding its customers by contradicting the statements in its prospectus. Funds have created disincentives to market timing through additional fees or even banning investors that engage in market timing. In this scandal, certain customers were exempted from these penalties, and the fund company explicitly or implicitly condoned their market timing. In fact, David Brown of the New York Attorney General's office discovered form-letter contracts between mutual fund companies and market timers (Swensen, 2005, p. 286). These practices demonstrated the difference between the organizations' stated rules and their practices as well as the preferential treatment afforded investors of a certain status.

The motivation for mutual fund companies to allow some investors to engage in late trading and market timing comes from the mutual fund's compensation scheme. Managers are paid based upon a percentage of total assets invested in the fund. The theory behind this incentive is that the best performing funds will attract the most money, so in order for a fund manager to maximize their income they must make sure that the fund maximizes its performance. It aligns with the ideology of the "free hand" or "market discipline" argument that economists have used since Adam Smith. In this case, hedge funds and other institutional investors subverted the spirit of the incentive system by investing a large amount in the mutual fund-maybe tens of millions of dollars-with the understanding that this investment would be for the long term and would allow fund managers to substantially increase their "assets under management". In exchange for the large investment, the fund manager would allow the investor to use a smaller account-perhaps one to five million dollars-to late trade and market time. This way, both parties benefited while the average investor loses by having profits skimmed from their investment.

Investors do not need to collude with the mutual fund to engage in market timing. Market timers are only detected after they have already made a number of trades. The difficulty in prevention is compounded because of difficulties in monitoring a large number of accounts and a general lack of transparency in mutual fund transactions. Because the market timing rule is only enforced by mutual fund companies, the fund faces a loss of business if it prevents an investor from market timing while another fund allows it, as the investor can transfer their assets to the second fund. While allowing mutual funds the ability to enforce their own market timing rules may allow them flexibility to make exceptions to the rule based upon the circumstances of each case, it also creates a conflict of interest that can create lax enforcement of these policies.

Theories of White-Collar Crime

The focus of this work is to provide a better understanding of the mutual fund scandal, its causes, prosecution, and means of prevention future abuses. These different areas are analyzed as they relate to the scandal and then used to inform larger discussions within the field of white-collar crime. This section examines the extant literature for understanding issues related to, prosecuting and regulating the market timing and late trading.

Causes of the Scandal

Causes of the scandal can be seen in terms of two overarching ingredients Coleman (1987) identified as essential to any crime: motivation and opportunity. Motivation may vary from individual to individual, making it difficult to determine the true motives of criminal acts. Coleman defines motivation as "a set of symbolic constructions defining certain kinds of goals and activities as appropriate and desirable and others as lacking those qualities (Coleman, 1987, p. 409)." Desirable goals and activities come from societal values, and in economies based on capitalism the element of competition is core value.

Competition

Coleman (1987) explains the culture of competition as a result of individuals' goals of wealth and success. These desires are exacerbated by an industrial capitalist society where a fear of failure permeates society and provides motivation for committing crime (Coleman, 1987, pp. 416-417). These two ideas of "success through wealth" and "non-failure" are distinct, but they work together in Coleman's discussion of motivation. Wheeler (1992) concludes that it is not always just greed, but sometimes a "fear of falling", or a potential loss in relative status, which motivates actors to engage in white-collar crime. Competition may also be considered part of the opportunity, as extreme competition can influence broker-dealers to search out the largest accounts in order to improve their own compensation. Findings from this scandal include a perversion of competition where sellers engage in illegal practices to increase their business.

Management Attitudes

Jenkins and Braithwaite (1993) noticed that white-collar crime literature repeatedly found pressure for the worst types of corporate crime coming from the organization's management. This pressure is then put upon the employees in different ways. Interview research with company executives consistently elicits the view that top management's attitudes, most particularly those of chief executives, determine the level of a corporation's compliance with the law (Clinard, 1983). Data on compliance with nursing home regulations confirmed that when pressure for profits is greatest, the boss is most likely to say, "This is the bottom line that I want. I don't care (and I don't want to know) what you have to do to get there (Jenkins & Braithwaite, 1993, p. 230)." Geis (1967) found that offenders convicted in the heavy electrical equipment antitrust cases testified that they were introduced to price-fixing practices by their bosses (Geis, 1967). This indicates that management motivates their employees to engage in crime by: creating a company attitude that condones crime, pushing employees for results regardless of the means, and/or directly introducing employees to illegal practices.

Opportunities

The importance of examining the structures of the mutual fund scandal is emphasized by Levi (1984). He notes that criminologists have obsessed over why people do what they do and have tended to neglect the equally important issue of how they are able to do what they do (Levi, 1984). The examination of opportunities includes how structures of the securities industry, mutual fund industry, and individual mutual funds allowed illegal practices to persist and, for a period of time, go undetected by regulators. This can be examined within the larger framework of Needleman and Needleman's (1979) work on environments that breed crime. They eschew previous notions that organizational environments "coerced" individuals to commit crimes. Instead, they argue that the organizational environment can create opportunities for crime, a condition they termed "crime-facilitative environments."

Needleman and Needleman argue that the coercive model does not explain why crime is not committed by all actors in such criminogenic environments. In the crime-facilitative model the environment does not compel employees to commit crimes, but rather, supplies tempting structural conditions for illegality including: high incentives, opportunities, and low risks. The Needlemans found that criminal activity is essential to business in a crime-coercive system. This is in contrast to a crime-facilitative system, where the criminal activity is an unavoidable cost of doing business.

The Needlemans discovered three crime-facilitative structural features in their study of fraudulent dealing in the securities industry: the pattern of legal liability, incentives for market flow, and the industry's traditions of commerce. The "traditions of commerce" refers to practices or structures in the securities industry that continue to exist even when technology or innovation has made them outdated. Traditions of commerce are relevant to the study of mutual fund fraud, because the mutual fund's pricing and order ticket process may be considered archaic traditions that make them vulnerable to fraud. For example, if computer technology was utilized to put prices in real-time, or to automate the order ticket process, this would lessen human involvement in the process, and could potentially reduce opportunities for collusion in late trading.

Prosecution Issues

Understanding how and why particular approaches were used in prosecuting these acts can help inform which factors influenced prosecutorial decision making for this scandal and how this relates to white-collar crime, in general. The mutual fund scandal resulted in dozens of cases being settled and over $5 billion in penalties paid by offenders and organizations, but few people were given prison sentences. It is important, from theoretical and policy standpoints, to understand why certain cases were pursued while others were not, as well as examining why particular types punishments were pursued over others.

Calavita and Pontell's (1994) analysis of the savings and loan prosecutions found that aggressive punishment of "thrift" offenders was conducted because it was an issue of "economic regulation" instead of "social regulation." They find that active enforcement of social regulation generally occurs in response to public pressure and concerns of legitimation. The stakes are higher where economic regulation is concerned, and the state is likely to take a more rigorous approach to offenses. Despite protests from those that face such sanctions, the state will more likely enforce regulations that stabilize the economy and enhance economic viability and investment. Economic regulations are central to a functioning economy and will be more consistently and vigorously enforced (Pontell, Rosoff, & Peterson, 2007). Over time the government's response to S&Ls shifted with the involvement of political actors whose careers were closely tied to thrift lobbyists. The government's response changed from "crime control" to "damage control" (Calavita & Pontell, 1995). The punishments in the mutual fund scandal also appear to have decreased over time. Further examination of the issue can help identify the cause of this decrease.

The Post-Enron Era and Public Reactions to White-Collar Crime

The fact that the mutual fund scandal occurred in the "Post-Enron Era" is important to understand how it was viewed by the public and subsequently treated by authorities. In reality, the mutual fund scandal may not have been a "scandal" if a number of corporate debacles had not occurred immediately before. One could also say that perhaps the most salient aspect of the mutual fund scandal was that it "failed to scandalize," in that it did not bring produce mass outrage from the millions of investors who – however slightly – were victimized, or by the government, the business community and lawmakers. A single prosecutor – Eliot Spitzer – was the primary force behind the making of these cases, and weathered considerable doubt and criticism from the public and the business community in doing so. Even if it had become a news story "with legs," the question remains as to whether it would have been prosecuted to the extent that it was – or at all, for that matter – in the pre-Enron era, given that only a few companies were involved in the initial case against Canary Capital Partners. Examining how this scandal was treated by the media compared to other recent financial debacles, could lead to a better understanding of the relationship between public reactions to white-collar crime and prosecutorial responses.

Braithwaite (1982) found that the community generally perceives many forms of white-collar crime as more serious, and deserving of more severe punishment, than most forms of common crime. Nevertheless, white-collar crimes which cause severe harm to persons are generally rated as more serious than all other types of crime and even some types of individual homicide. While people might be in favor of directing fire and thunder at white-collar criminals in the abstract, when confronted with a remorseful businessman in the dock who puts forth some plausible rationalizations for his wrongs, condemnation mellows (Braithwaite, 1982, p. 738). This is supported by Grabosky, Braithwaite, and Wilson, (1987) whose study of public perceptions of crime find that white-collar crimes that cause severe harm to persons are generally rated as more serious than all other types of crime and even some types of individual homicide (pp. 42-43). While this indicates that the public considers white-collar offenses to be serious crimes, many empirical studies have found that leniency prevails in the sanctioning of white-collar criminals (Calavita, Pontell, & Tillman, 1997; Hagan & Nagel, 1982; Hagan, Nagel, & Albonetti, 1980; Tillman & Pontell, 1992).

Difficulties in Prosecution

This disjuncture between public attitudes and prosecutorial response may be understood through research on the difficulties of prosecuting white-collar offenses. The literature supports the view that complex evidence and the capacity of wealthy defendants to mobilize legal talent makes prosecuting white-collar offenders more difficult (Levi, 1981). Shapiro (1985) examined the notion of differential treatment between securities violations cases and common crimes. She traces the SEC enforcement process in which most stock swindlers are diverted from criminal prosecution and treated civilly, administratively, or spared legal action entirely. Her findings indicate that the most significant offenses attract the criminal process, but also those about which little else can be done. In this light, her thesis reconsiders the controversial finding that upper status white-collar offenders fare no better and often worse than their lower status counterparts at criminal sentencing.

Shapiro found that disinclination for criminal prosecution comes from: criminal procedure being more technically difficult; increased consumption of resources; and the ability of SEC to implement their own civil or administrative options, (Shapiro, 1985, p. 181). Offense seriousness trumps any status consideration for determining prosecutorial action. However, if seriousness is controlled, status and social context of the violation do account for variability.

Goetz (1997) believes that Shapiro's examination of the sentencing of white-collar offenders ignores modern conceptions of power and bias. In his work on arson for profit, Goetz argues that power is found on multiple dimensions, and bias manifests itself in different ways. Shapiro's findings show that class-bias is a minor factor in sentencing, but Goetz believes this is because her analysis ignores more subtle representations of power and bias that exist in the case of white-collar crime. Shapiro's analysis uses a one-dimensional power analysis, which seeks direct evidence of organized interests exerting their influence on organizational structures and processes. Two-dimensional and three-dimensional power analyses assume that institutions operate systematically to promote certain groups and state structures work to sustain capitalist growth and mitigate public issues that reflect social inequalities[2] (Lukes, 1974).

In the case of arson-for-profit, law enforcement agencies made arson a "non-issue" altogether by refusing to recognize the possibility that it was motivated by fraud from real estate developers and landlords. This non-action by the arson agency classified the cases as common crime and eliminated the possibility of white-collar crime being considered at all, while simultaneously controlling the discourse about the issue.

In terms of the ability to utilize the resources necessary to prosecute all these cases, the fact that the scandal came about in the "post-Enron" environment may have meant that more resources were devoted to handling these cases. System capacity in criminal justice concerns the ability of the system to afford the money, time, and other legal resources needed to process offenders (Pontell, 1984). In the case of white-collar crime, the term has been slightly adapted as "institutional capacity", which reflects a combination of environmental and internal organizational constraints, including legal barriers, resource limitations, failures of inter-organizational coordination and cooperation, and the beliefs and practices of agents themselves, which all work together to either enhance or hinder the ability to discover and deter white-collar criminality (Pontell, 1984; Levi, 1987; Black, Calavita, & Pontell, 1995; Pontell et al., 1994).

Insight into the SEC

Shapiro spent a total of ten and a half months at SEC offices. This included nine months going through case archives and six weeks interviewing personnel and observing how SEC offices function (Shapiro, 1984, p. 194). Shapiro found that particular types of crimes were more likely to be discovered and investigated by SEC agents. For example, approximately 95% of offenses detected through market surveillance were either market manipulation or self-dealing cases (Shapiro, 1984, p. 104). This is consistent with the nature of these types of crimes, as they are committed on stock exchanges, leaving artifacts detected through regulatory observation rather than disclosure or victim reporting. Disclosure by insiders is ineffectual for these types of crime, because manipulation or self-dealing may be committed by individuals who do not share details with others. Victim reporting is equally weak with these cases, as many victims often do not realize they were victimized (Rosoff, Pontell, & Tillman, 2006). Therefore, if market surveillance were the sole strategy being used, regulators would almost exclusively discover these two types of crime. Knowing this, it is difficult to infer why market timing and late trading were not detected by regulators' use of market surveillance, as these crimes were also forms of self-dealing. Of course, it is not known how much time and effort were placed into proactive or reactive intelligence gathering strategies, which may explain regulatory agencies' failure to discover the mutual fund scandal. Also, illegal mutual fund trades were obscured due to an absence of laws and regulations requiring transparency in mutual fund trades, which would have made it easier for the SEC to identify offending investors. This problem has since been addressed by SEC rule 22c-2 which forces financial intermediaries to supply mutual fund companies with information regarding which clients are making trades and how often those trades are being made (SEC, 9/30/04).

Shapiro's finding that the organization of the SEC's intelligence apparatus determines which types of violations it detects, is consistent with enforcement patterns from the mutual fund scandal. In this case, the SEC did not consider mutual funds to be high risk areas and reduced the quantity and quality of their mutual fund audits.

> Prior to September 2003, SEC staff did not examine for market timing abuses or assess company controls over that

activity because agency staff (1) viewed market timing as a relatively low-risk area that did not involve per se violations; (2) determined that mutual fund companies had financial incentives to establish effective controls over frequent trading because such trading can reduce fund returns resulting in a loss of business; and (3) were told by company officials that they had designated compliance staff to monitor and control market timing (Government Accountability Office [GAO], 2005c, p. 4).

By focusing on mutual fund managerial decision-making and theft opportunities the SEC missed opportunities to prevent market timing and late trading through audits. This demonstrates that the SEC's organization of its intelligence apparatus not only determines which types of violations it will detect, but also which violations are likely to go undetected.

This notion can be combined with other theories of regulation to give us a better understanding of why the regulatory system has failed in certain cases. The term "system capacity", in the criminal justice context, concerns the justice system's ability to expend the money, time, and other legal resources needed to process offenders (Pontell, 1984). With white-collar crime, the term has been slightly adapted as "institutional capacity", which reflects a combination of environmental and internal organizational constraints, including legal barriers, resource limitations, failures of inter-organizational coordination and cooperation, and the beliefs and practices of agents themselves, which all work together to either enhance or hinder the ability to discover and deter white-collar criminality (Pontell, 1984; Levi, 1987; Black, Calavita, & Pontell, 1995; Pontell et al., 1994).

The inability to cover all areas is exacerbated by limited resources, which prevent the SEC from covering their blind spots. Once alternative methods expose the violations and blind spots as in the case of the mutual fund scandal, the agency is forced to make strategic decisions regarding how to shift resources. The only redress for this situation seems to be for the SEC to gain more resources; or to be able to predict where violations are likely to occur and prevent them. While there is no record of the latter there is good news regarding the former. The SEC had a 125+% budget increase in the wake of corporate accounting and mutual fund scandals. In 2003 the SEC budget increased over 100% from the previous year from $44 to $100 million

(GAO, 2004). The SEC's ability to utilize resources necessary to prosecute these cases may have been aided by the fact that the mutual fund scandal came about in the "post-Enron". However, it is difficult to estimate how much would be enough to provide complete protection for investors. As no one knows the actual amount of fraud occurring in the corporate and financial worlds, it is impossible to estimate how large a budget would be needed to thoroughly prevent, detect, and investigate these offenses given both their nature and the availability of evidence.

To further complicate matters Shapiro reported a high personnel turnover rate within the SEC, noting, "Many of those I encountered were young, briefly passing through the agency on their way to private practice (Shapiro, 1984, p. 141)." She also noted how cases would regularly last months or years. This implies that turnover could negatively affect SEC investigation and prosecution of cases, as those SEC agents actively working on cases move on to other careers. This could cause problems as departing agents' caseloads are distributed to other employees. It also involves large amounts of resources in training new employees causing the agency to effectively operate below its maximum enforcement capacity. In sum, high turnover rates of SEC agents causes disruption to the normal flow of cases, consumes agency resources through training new employees, and negatively affects efficiency in terms of fraud prevention and control.

The GAO believes that the SEC suffers from system capacity limitations similar to those described by Pontell (1984), and it suggested that the SEC improve its institutional capacity, in order to better understand threats to investors (GAO, 2005c). These findings, combined with Shapiro's, create a negative outlook regarding the SEC's mission. This leaves limited resources, forcing the SEC to select intelligence gathering strategies which are not exhaustive to all types of corporate and financial crimes leaving enforcement blind spots that allow other types of crimes to go unnoticed. Within the last decade this regulatory situation has been verified by eventual and quite prominent "non-discoveries" all of which have resulted in major financial scandals.

These "non-discoveries" are found in cases such as Enron, WorldCom, Adelphia, and dozens of other corporations that were brought to public attention through the actions of whistleblowers. While these were largely cases of accounting fraud, and therefore more difficult to detect through proactive measures, the lack of oversight from regulatory organizations provided opportunity for these corporate executives to offend without risk of being detected. In fact, it was discovered that the SEC had not audited Enron for three years prior to their company imploding from massive fraud (McManus, 2/3/03). Even though corporate accounting cases were difficult to discover through proactive measures, there were several other large scandals that lent themselves to such enforcement practice had it occurred.

Cases of fraud or misrepresentation by stock analysts and research firms created a major scandal in the securities industry, which was discovered by Eliot Spitzer. In fact, it has been identified as one of the causes for the stock bubble of the 1990's and subsequent crash of the early 2000's. While Alan Greenspan's famously termed this cause of the crash as investors' "irrational exuberance", their exuberance was actually fairly rational as they were only reacting to information supplied by analysts and firms. The problem is the firms and analysts had been corrupted (Lehrer, 12/6/96). In this scandal, analysts were giving positive recommendations regarding stocks that they had either not fully evaluated or where they ignored potential red flags. In exchange for giving positive ratings, analysts received gifts, money, and other forms of compensation from their firms. Citigroup, for example, was never formally charged by Spitzer, although they did settle for $400 million after it was discovered that Citigroup CEO Sanford Weill had convinced their telecom analyst to give AT&T stock a higher rating. In exchange, Weill helped the analyst get his children into an exclusive Manhattan nursery school. Weill was putting pressure on the analyst in the hope of winning investment banking business for Citigroup (Hamilton, 7/17/03). Also, companies being evaluated would manipulate relationships with analysts either through pleading for a positive rating or threatening to cut-off access-which would threaten an analyst's livelihood. A survey published in the *Journal of Managerial Issues* reported that 61% of analysts had been threatened about negative research (USA Today, 3/24/02). The obvious conflicts of interest and consistent positive reports in the face of down markets should have been obvious signals to the SEC of problems in this industry.

The mutual fund scandal represents the third major scandal that the SEC failed to detect within a few years time. As previously noted, market timing and late trading cases were exposed by a company insider who chose to approach Eliot Spitzer rather than the SEC (Elkind, 4/19/04). As in previous scandals, the SEC investigated the abuses only after they had been reported elsewhere. They also managed to negotiate several large settlements including some of the largest ever reached with the SEC (GAO, 2005c).

The one exception to this pattern of SEC failures is a number of insider trading cases that were detected and settled through SEC offices. Between 2001 and 2006, the SEC has brought over 300 actions against more than 600 individuals and organizations, which represents just approximately 10% of the SEC's total caseload during that period (Thomsen, 9/26/06). This makes investigating and prosecuting insider trading cases a significant part of the SEC's workload.

Insider trading is a unique crime because it is conducted in an extremely public forum which is highly scrutinized; stock exchanges. Due to the immense quantity of money changing hands, the type of suspicious trading that suggests insider trading is more easily noticed than accounting fraud due to the evidence left from stock trades. In accounting fraud numbers are produced internally and supported by colluding auditors based on proprietary information, so there are fewer chances for artifacts to remain and provide evidence of fraud.

Ironically, market timing in mutual funds is more similar to insider trading than accounting fraud, while late trading is more similar to accounting fraud. The nature of insider trading makes it more identifiable. It is usually tied to advance knowledge of some kind of company announcement, so regulators can backtrack from any major announcements to identify irregular trading activity for a particular security. However, there is no evidence that regulators do similar financial forensic work with mutual funds even though they are affected by the same stock announcements that would signal insider trading. Late trading would be more difficult due to cover-ups which make such trades look legitimate.

In addition to problems detecting scandals, the SEC has been roundly criticized by state agencies for their lack of retributive punishments against white-collar offenders. Shapiro found that 85% of documented investigations uncovered a violation. Almost half resulted in no formal legal action against the offender. Of cases that did not involve any formal legal action, about one-third were referred to self-regulatory agencies, a quarter received informal sanctions, and 9% were referred to other agencies (Shapiro, 1984, chap. 6).

It is possible that Shapiro's analysis should be reconsidered in light of the GAO's findings that the SEC is lax in making referrals to other agencies; especially if this situation existed during the time of her research. The GAO examined SEC files related to mutual fund cases and found that the files often had missing or incomplete notes regarding the resolutions of SEC investigations. Specifically, the SEC did not record whether referrals to other agencies were or were not made. Consequently, the report's primary recommendation was that the SEC keep better records of which cases were referred to prosecutors (GAO, 2005b). A degradation of the SEC's record keeping quality may have been expected as the agency's workload has increased dramatically over the past three decades, while their staff has grown at a much slower rate. However, the SEC justified these procedures by saying that formal criminal referral procedures were too time consuming and not effective (GAO, 2005c). Whether or not this is true, it hinders others from trying to evaluate the SEC's effectiveness.

Understanding how the SEC justifies decision-making is valuable for several reasons. An organization that reviews its decisions and employee performance over a period of time, understands what it does well and where it could improve. It could also serve a legal purpose. While it unknown what reviews the SEC undertook in the wake of the market timing and late trading scandal, the SEC had received tips from mutual fund insiders that market timing offenses were being allowed to proliferate within mutual fund companies. These same companies later reached settlements with Spitzer's office and the SEC regarding these very same offenses.

Outside of micro-level justifications for non-action on individual cases, there are structural factors which reduce the number of SEC cases that end up in criminal trials. According to Shapiro, disinclination for criminal prosecution comes from: criminal procedure being more technically difficult; criminal procedure taking up more resources; or SEC officials implementing their own civil or administrative options (Shapiro, 1985). These findings have been supported through research from others and have been generalized to be relevant to other forms of white-collar crime (Braithwaite, 1985; Calavita & Pontell, 1994; Wheeler, Mann, & Sarat, 1988).

Despite the focus on justifications for cases that were not prosecuted, examining the number of cases that were prosecuted and large sums that were extracted in fines and disgorgements is valuable to understanding how much value the SEC placed on these cases. Shapiro commented that she had been very impressed by the amount of in-depth discussion that took place among SEC managers regarding enforcement recommendations (Shapiro, 1984, pp. 151-152).

Assuming this is still the case, the SEC must have considered these cases to be important. The other possibility is that the SEC perceived these cases as important to the agency's image, and it did not want to lose public confidence.

Regardless of why the SEC placed importance on mutual fund cases, the punishments issued demonstrate that they did make these cases a priority. The GAO analyzed SEC punishments in mutual fund cases. At the time of their study, the SEC had imposed fourteen actions against mutual fund companies and ten actions against other types of firms. Penalties ranged from $2 million to $140 million, and averaged $56 million, which is well under the $20 million average for SEC penalties. These penalties extended to individuals as well. Enforcement actions were brought against 24 individuals, and the SEC obtained penalties and industry bars in all of these cases and disgorgements in some. Settlements ranged from $40 thousand to $30 million. In fact, the three highest penalties were $30 million and two were for $20 million. These cases represented three of the four highest penalties obtained from individuals in SEC history (GAO, 2005c).

The GAO found that the SEC used a formula in determining penalties that was consistent with other cases against investment advisers. They also found that the agency coordinated these actions and sanctions with interested state regulatory agencies. A three-tiered system of punishment is established for the SEC to apply for offenders. The first tier is $65,000 for organizations and $6,500 for individuals per violation, the second tier is $325,000 for organizations and $65,000 for individuals per violation and the third tier is $650,000 for organizations and $130,000 for individuals per violations (GAO, 2005b). The severity of penalties the SEC applied to mutual fund offenders is directly related to this scale. The SEC Director of Enforcement specifically said that the relatively high penalties in these cases are part of an effort to increase accountability and enhance deterrence in the securities industry. However, the SEC did not necessarily follow maximum penalty guidelines, as listed above. As the GAO report discusses, if the SEC had imposed the maximum possible penalty in one of their cases, the offending company would have been fined approximately $1 billion dollars, due to the number of violations which were discovered. Although the actual settlement of this case was not given, no fine exceeded $330 million. The SEC sought a penalty much lower than $1 billion dollars because they perceived relatively little harm done to investors, as well as a lack of full awareness by the offenders. SEC staff also believed that imposing such a high penalty would have eliminated the possibility of settling the case; besides, a judge likely would have found the proposed penalty inappropriate for the crime.

Regulation and Punishment

The mutual fund industry is a vital part of many American's retirement savings. As pensions and other company sponsored retirement plans are discontinued, Americans may be relying more heavily upon the mutual fund industry to fund their retirement. For this reason, the industry must maintain a reputation for integrity and safety, so that legitimacy is maintained in the financial system and the larger economy. This makes reform a salient issue in establishing investor confidence in mutual funds and ensuring that the current scandal does not repeat itself. The SEC proposed several reforms to reduce the likelihood of future late trading and market timing, but many of these proposals have met with considerable resistance from the mutual funds and associated organizations. Understanding the different viewpoints on the issue of mutual fund reform helps inform larger arguments over economic and financial regulation.

Neo-Classical Economics

The neo-classical economic theories used to regulate the securities industry have focused on the "invisible hand" or market discipline to control the ability of actors to commit crimes within the industry. Nobel-prize winning economist Milton Friedman long advocated this view that the corporation remains singularly focused on profits while regulation interferes with this legal mandate (Friedman, 1962). Easterbrook and Fischel's (1991) work establishes the modern economic philosophies used to justify free market approaches to regulation. These arguments discount the empirical findings of collusion in the Savings & Loan scandal, the Insider Trading Scandals, and the mutual fund scandals. Criminologists have found that policies based on neo-classical economic theories have created crime-facilitative structures while decreasing the likelihood of crime detection (Black, 2005; Pontell, 2004). A similar result can be found in the preliminary analysis of how a lack of transparency and conflicts of interest in fund governance facilitated crime in mutual funds. Further study in this area provides a better understanding of which theories of regulation have failed, and why increased economic and financial regulation may reduce white-collar criminality.

Responsive Regulation

Ayres and Braithwaite (1992) developed "responsive regulation" which seeks to have governments or private actors vary their regulatory response based upon the severity of the offense and the likely success of a particular type of approach (restorative justice, deterrence, or incapacitation). They believe responsive regulation can cover the weaknesses of any one punishment theory, with the strengths of the other two. In order to do this, Ayers and Braithwaite created a "pyramid of regulation" that recommends regulators begin with the base of least punitive and move their way up to most punitive, if the act is very serious or if modest punishments have failed (Ayres & Braithwaite, 1992; see Appendix 2). This, however, places an emphasis on specific deterrence and maximizing resources over retribution, and may not make amends for damage caused by the action in question. This could allow actors to know that they have a certain leeway to offend as long as they stop before their punishment escalates past a certain point. There may also be issues determining which offenses qualify as severe. Responsive regulation is the opposite of "regulatory formalism" which pre-determines the type of regulatory response regardless of the offense. Braithwaite (2002) posits that while responsive regulation may lack consistency, in terms of an ideology of punishment, regulatory formalism will regularly cause us to make things worse for future victims of the wrongdoing (Braithwaite, 2002, pp. 29-30). However, as presented, responsive regulation is a form of pre-determined punishment. The problem that Braithwaite presents for pre-determined punishments are the same problems that responsive regulation may face, and will always be a problem when priorities are set for determining punishment. Responsive regulation tries to escape some of these issues by making the pre-determination more fluid, but with that much fluidity its implementation will be subject to different managerial influences and preferences.

Legal-Pluralist Models of Regulation

Braithwaite (1995) uses a legal-pluralist model of regulation to understand why prospects for protecting the public interest from exploitation by pharmaceutical transnationals are actually improving. He contends that intervention is meant to protect the public interest at a number of levels: national regulatory enforcement, regional regulatory cooperation, international regulatory coordination, intrafirm regulation through both individual executive consciences (internal compliance groups), interfirm self-regulation through national and international industry associations as well as through the work of reforming individual firms, and private regulation by product liability suits and consumer activism (Braithwaite, 1995, p. 302). This legal-pluralism is utilized to understand the response to the mutual fund scandal, especially as to how state, federal, and private regulatory agencies joined together to prosecute cases in the scandal.

Legal-pluralist policy is similar to responsive regulation in that both believe there are constructive ways of solving problems of lawbreaking and evasion without immediate recourse to the criminal law. This allows the government to harbor their criminal enforcement resources for the few cases where criminal prosecution is the best way to respond. Fisse and Braithwaite's accountability model proposes that having proved the *actus reus* of the offense, the court would invite the corporation to prepare, perhaps with outside consultants, a report indicating the reasons for the offense, those responsible for its execution, the organizational reforms to be taken to prevent recurrence, and the disciplinary measures to be taken against those responsible. If the package of measures is satisfactory to the needs of justice and community protection, then criminal sanctioning is withheld (Fisse & Braithwaite, 1993).

Currently, regulatory agencies may resist prosecuting guilty parties in order to gain their cooperation in safeguarding public health (Braithwaite, 1982, p. 751). This can be seen in the adjudication of unsafe products, where official threats may force voluntary self-regulation and recalls while prosecution may induce companies to try and hide their guilt. This helps us understand why regulatory agencies limited criminal sanctions after they investigated the mutual fund scandal. Fisse and Braithwaite showed with their seventeen case studies that white-collar crime scandals often produced substantial preventive reform prior to or even in the absence of convictions (Fisse & Braithwaite, 1983). Waldman's studies of the impact of antitrust prosecution showed that some of the most dramatic changes in the competitiveness of markets occurred where the government failed to secure convictions (Waldman, 1978).

Notes

1 "Short-selling" refers to the investment strategy of betting that the investment vehicle will decrease in value. In order to carry this out with a stock, the investor must borrow the stock from the brokerage firm and then sell it. The investor then "owes" the brokerage firm that much of the company's stock. The investor keeps the cash, but must buy back the same quantity of stock at a later date to fulfill their obligation. If the stock decreases in value after the sale, the investor can buy back the stock and keep the difference. If the stock increases in value, the investor can buy back the stock, but must supply the cash to cover the difference. It is important to note that it is not illegal to short-sell a mutual fund, but it is virtually impossible to do without the illegal sharing of mutual fund information. Since it is a collection of investment vehicles bundled together, the mutual fund itself cannot be short sold. The only way to short-sell a mutual fund would be to have access to the mutual fund's actual holdings and then short-sell shares of those securities in quantities equivalent to that of the mutual fund. The SEC only requires a mutual fund to make its holdings public twice a year, but that information is known for being outdated at its time of publication. This meant that Stern had to convince the mutual fund companies to give him access to insider information regarding the mutual fund's current holding and trading activities.

2 A two-dimensional view of power assumes that governmental structures and processes themselves represent a "mobilization of bias," where "institutional procedures operate systematically and consistently to the benefit of certain persona and groups at the expense of others" (Lukes, 1974, pp. 16-17)...A three dimensional view of power, according to Lukes (1974, p. 53), is similar to a two-dimensional view. But it has less to do with the ways that public organizations respond to the reputations of elites, especially within the context of particular issues, and more to do with analyzing the ways that state structures and processes systematically work to both sustain capitalist growth and mitigate (however unsuccessfully) the emergence of public issues that reflect social inequities (Lukes, 1974; Offe, 1974; O'Connor, 1973; Poulantzas, 1969).

CHAPTER 2

Cases from the Mutual Fund Scandal

This chapter seeks to explore some of the commonalities and exceptions among late trading and market timing cases which comprised this series of events known as the mutual fund scandal. The discussion will primarily be split into two sections. The first covers aspects of offenders and offenses committed, while the second section compares punishments issued by the various regulatory agencies. The issue of punishments will be examined with regard to larger theories of white-collar crime, while the actual punishments and their justifications will be explored more thoroughly in subsequent chapters that concentrate on individual regulatory agencies. For example, this chapter spends a lot of time examining trends of punishments over time, while subsequent chapters will more thoroughly address the methodologies used for determining sanctions as well as unique aspects of punishment which were common to one group or another.

There is no one single offending pattern among cases from the market timing and late trading mutual fund scandal. Included in this group are: fraud by management, fraud by employees, fraud by outsiders, collusion between multiple groups, independent actions by outside actors, clearly illegal actions, questionably illegal actions. In the aggregate, however, each case represents endemic practices in the mutual fund industry that benefited a select few investors while robbing from the majority.

Former SEC Chairman, Arthur Levitt, described the mutual fund scandal in harsh terms. "This is far and away the most serious and pervasive scandal to hit America's markets in the past century. The ethical loss is cataclysmic (PBS, 11/26/03)." While the ethical loss may have been substantial, the monetary loss was also dramatic. There were approximately 66 cases involving market timing and/or late trading in which some sort of punishment was issued. These punishments included: criminal sanctions, civil fines, banning of employees from the securities industry by a regulatory agency, or company-imposed broker firings. These 66 cases resulted in over 120 firings, 10 criminal convictions, over $2.6 billion in disgorgement, almost $1.5 billion in organizational fines, and over $5.4 billion in total penalties. Civil fines represented the large majority of market timing and late trading cases. Included in civil penalties are several combinations of organizational fines, individual fines, disgorgement of profits earned from market timing and/or late trading, and fee reductions. Fee reductions will be discussed more thoroughly in later chapters, but this was a penalty commonly imposed by Eliot Spitzer and the New York State Attorney General's office.

Offenses, Offenders, and Trends

Criminal Cases

While the majority of news attention focused on the civil cases and their large financial penalties, there were at least eleven criminal cases that either went to trial or resulted in plea bargains. Of these eleven cases, ten resulted in convictions, all from plea bargains. The one criminal case that went to trial resulted in a hung jury and the case was never re-tried.

The ten criminal convictions were all plea agreements on various charges. The first case involved former Vice Chairman and Chief Mutual Fund Officer, James P. Connelly, Jr., of Fred Alger & Company. He pleaded guilty to tampering with evidence, a class E felony, punishable by up to four years in prison. According to Eliot Spitzer and the SEC, who brought criminal and civil charges simultaneously, Connelly repeatedly attempted to thwart the investigation. He lied to his own company's lawyers to prevent them from discovering and producing documents subpoenaed by the New York Attorney General's office and related to the fund's illicit trading schemes. Connelly also ordered employees to delete emails and coached them to supply false information related to the market timing arrangements between Alger and Veras Investments, a Texas hedge fund. He was ultimately sentenced to 1 to 3 years in prison (New York

Office of the Attorney General [NYAOG], 10/16/03). According to the federal civil charges brought by the SEC, which Connelly settled for $400,000, he had been involved in approving timing arrangements since the mid-1990's (SEC, 10/16/03).

Other criminal cases from the late trading and market timing scandal included: James Wilson, a Trautman Wasserman broker, for a violation of New York's Martin Act/General Business Law. Stephen Burton, a former Assistant Vice-President of US Trust, pleaded guilty to destroying evidence related to the mutual fund investigation, a misdemeanor. Steven Markovitz, a former executive and senior trader at the hedge fund Millenium Partners, pleaded guilty to a violation of New York's Martin Act/General Business Law and received five years probation. Delano Santa Ana and Lawrence Powell, brokers at Kaplan Securities, both pleaded guilty to violations of New York's Martin Act/General Business Law. Grant Seeger, Nicole McDermott, and William Kenyon, the former CEO, the former Vice President of Corporate Services, and the former President of Security Trust Company pleaded guilty to different combinations of criminal charges. Seeger pleaded guilty to Second Degree Grand Larceny and a violation of New York's Martin Act/General Business Law, while Kenyon and McDermott pleaded guilty to a violation of New York's Martin Act/General Business Law. Finally, former head trader and owner of Securities Brokerage, Inc., William Calugar pleaded guilty to a violation of New York's Martin Act/General Business Law, after entering into secret agreement to market time with Franklin Templeton.

Paul Flynn, a former managing director for CIBC, was charged with five felonies, including grand larceny, as part of a scheme to finance market timing within the CIBC funds. The belief was that he arranged financing for Canary Capital and Samaritan Asset Management to conduct illegal trades, as part of the arrangement between the two hedge funds and Security Trust Co. to late trade mutual funds. The charges carried a maximum twenty-five year sentence. However, they were later dropped, as was the civil case brought by the SEC, before the criminal case went to trial. Flynn then sued CIBC for defamation and illegal termination. Ultimately, CIBC settled with him out of court for an undisclosed sum (Forbes, 11/28/08).

Since then, both Franklin Templeton and CIBC have been the subject of civil suits from investors. In the Summer of 2010, Franklin Templeton and two other Canadian mutual funds settled class action suits from investors based upon the funds allowing for market timing for large investors only.   There is another pending class action suit in Canada which names Franklin Templeton and two divisions of CIBC (Middlemiss, 9/22/2010).

The only criminal case to go to trial was that of Theodore Sihpol III, a former Bank of America broker who was accused of negotiating late trading access for Canary Capital with Bank of America's "Fund of Nations" mutual fund. Spitzer and company originally indicted Sihpol on forty counts ranging from Grand Larceny in the First Degree, a class B felony, to a violation of the General Business Law, a class E felony, although only thirty-three charges were carried over to the trial. The original charges carried a possible maximum of fifteen to thirty years in prison.   At the trial's end, twenty-nine of the original thirty-three charges were dismissed by the State Supreme Court of Manhattan, and the jury was hung on the remaining four charges. Those charges were never re-filed by Eliot Spitzer-who by that point was running for Governor of New York (Atlas & Abelson, 6/10/05). The remaining four charges consisted of securities fraud, scheming to defraud, and two counts of falsifying business records.

The SEC brought federal civil charges against Sihpol at the same time the criminal complaint was filed. In October 2005 they settled their case for $400,000 and prohibition from working in the securities industry for a period of five years (Moyer, 10/12/05).

Despite the lack of a conviction, people privy to the details of this case believe Sihpol and Bank of America were heavily involved in illegal activities. According to Eddie Stern, Bank of America (BoA) was one of the most active and most clearly illegal relationships that Canary Capital cultivated (Elkind, 4/19/04). Stern claims that the connection was established in April 2001, when BoA private client services broker, Theodore Sihpol III, visited Eddie Stern at Canary's office, inquiring about Stern's interest in trading mutual funds through BoA. Stern explained Canary's market timing practices and the results that he had earned up to that point. Sihpol tried to get approvals from BoA for Canary's trading schemes, and invited Stern to make a presentation of his market timing strategies to a group of bank employees, including members of BoA's clearing division. This meeting took place in late April 2001 (Elkind, 4/19/04). After the presentation, BoA allegedly offered their "Nations Fund" for Canary to do market timing, a $300 million credit line, lists of their mutual fund portfolios to facilitate mutual fund short selling, and Canary's own electronic trading terminal so that Canary could late trade mutual funds directly. This platform allowed Canary to late trade with any of the fund families in BoA's clearing system until 6:30pm of that trading day (Elkind, 4/19/04).

Bank of America representatives appeared very aware and complicit in this arrangement. Sihpol received written confirmation for Canary's market timing and late trading schemes from his boss, Charles Bryceland; the BoA clearing division compliance representative; and the investment manager of the Nations Funds. The clearing division's compliance manager questioned the propriety of this arrangement until Sihpol told him that other BoA employees "felt the business was worthwhile and an appropriate use of [BoA] resources (Brown, New York Supreme Court Complaint)." In addition, Bryceland sent an email congratulating all those involved in building the relationship with Canary including: Sihpol, the private lending department, and the Nations fund executive who "[gave] access...for market timing activities". He concludes, "It is always nice to enter a new year with a success like this (Elkind, 4/19/04)." In September 2003, BoA fired Bryceland for his involvement in the mutual fund scandal (Atlas, 9/12/03). According to the civil complaint against Stern and Canary, "Canary made tens of millions through late trading and timing, while the various parts of Bank of America that serviced Canary made millions themselves (Brown, New York Supreme Court Complaint)."

Civil Cases

Outside of the ten criminal convictions and a few dismissed cases, there were at least sixty-two civil cases that were settled out of court with fines and/or special conditions for the offending individual or organization. These charges include: market timing, late trading, supervisory failures related to market timing and/or late trading, negotiated market timing and/or late trading, facilitating market timing and/or late trading, and deceptive market timing.

The differences between these offenses represent differences in the degree of involvement and intent in the illegal actions. For example, "negotiated" is considered more severe than "facilitating," which is more severe than "supervisory failures related to" in these types of crimes. Negotiated market timing and/or late trading refers to a situation where two separate organizations – usually a broker-dealer or hedge fund and a mutual fund – have an agreement where the broker/dealer or hedge fund is allowed to illegally trade in the mutual fund. In exchange, the mutual fund receives some type of benefit – usually in the form of "sticky assets" that temporarily boost the fund's financial sheet and increase compensation for the fund manager. In addition, there may be stipulations regarding how many illegal trades the first party may make, or how much in sticky assets they must deposit. The intent and high degree of complicity is why negotiated market timing and/or late trading cases were generally punished more severely than non-negotiated cases.

Cases of "facilitating market timing and/or late-trading" represent instances when the mutual fund would actively allow an entity to market time in their fund without necessarily including a pre-arranged agreement between the two entities. This represents a lesser degree of malice than negotiated market timing, because facilitated illegal trading does not necessarily require the pre-meditation of a negotiated trading agreement. However, it does require that the mutual fund has knowledge that market timing or late trading is occurring.

The final category, supervisory failures related to market timing were charged against organizations, usually in conjunction with findings of market timing in the organization. In these cases, there was no discovery of intent or malice from the mutual fund company. Instead, the regulator was only able to find that the organization had no internal controls in place to safeguard against investors illegally trading a fund. Whether or not more severe violations occurred, this represents a mutual fund's violation of their prospectus and a breach of trust against their investors, as the mutual fund company was responsible with policing their fund against market timing.

Another category of offense, which only applied to broker-dealers, includes deceptive market timing. This occurs when a broker-dealer actively attempts to hide illegal trading in the mutual fund company-deceptive late trading does not exist, because, due to its nature, late trading is always deceptive. Deceptive market timing infers that the mutual fund company had no knowledge of the illegal activity, and may have been trying to actively combat it. Some methods that broker-dealers used to accomplish deceptive market timing during this scandal, included: splitting up large trades so that they are less likely to be detected, creating multiple accounts under different names to hide the identities of the account owner making the trades, and creating multiple entities to process trades so that it appears as though these illegal trades are coming from different organizations (Elkind, 4/19/04).

Collaboration

Much of Spitzer's success settling cases was due to collaborative efforts during the entire scandal, with the SEC, NASD/FINRA, and other state attorney general's all involved in multiple settlements of mutual fund cases. Public announcements of cases were consistently described as "joint settlements" or "brought in conjunction with," and the SEC announcements all thanked the efforts of Spitzer's office, and/or whichever state-level regulator or self-regulatory body aided in developing and prosecuting the case.

Despite this multi-agency approach, or, as Braithwaite (1993) termed it, a legal-pluralist model of regulation, all criminal cases involved the New York State Attorney General's office. However, it is difficult to categorize this as proof Spitzer was acting outside of the legal-pluralist approach, as the SEC and those involved SROs are only legally permitted to bring civil cases or administrative cases against organizations or individuals. This would have prevented them from joining with Spitzer in his criminal cases. However, the SEC is allowed to make criminal referrals to the Department of Justice for specific cases, and there is a possibility that there could be some collaboration between state and federal prosecutors in terms of information sharing (E.G. Osterman, personal communication, 7/23/08).

Salient Issues Emerging from Case Studies

The following cases are examples of offenders and offenses committed during the late trading and market timing scandal. The objective is to demonstrate how the various illegal actions described above manifested themselves within organizations, often resulting in collusion between different groups. All of the cases discussed below resulted in some type of punitive sanction, either a criminal conviction, civil sanction, in-house disciplinary action, or some combination of the three. They focus on illegal actions that were discovered by the various regulatory agencies investigating the scandal-although many charges remain "alleged" as the majority of offenders entered into civil settlements that allowed them to neither admit nor deny any charges levied against them. Issues of punishment and prosecution will be discussed in later chapters, and will include more extensive examinations of those regulatory organizations involved in this scandal. Characteristics described here will include: specific actions of broker-dealers, mutual funds, and hedge funds; illegal arrangements and collusion between multiple parties; and which parties within organizations were involved in illegal trading.

One-Stop Shysters

The issue of how different parties conducted their illegal, late trades emerged from investigations and prosecutions of mutual fund cases. For most firms this involved some type of collusion, as was seen in the Security Trust Co. case, which resulted in the Office of the Comptroller of Currency forcing the company to dissolve, due to their involvement in this scandal. In that case, Canary Capital solicited the assistance of Security Trust in helping disguise illegal trades by allowing them to be processed after the 4 pm deadline, then treating them as normal orders, therefore eliminating a key level of oversight in mutual fund order processing. However, other organizations were large enough that they contained their own order processing in-house, which allowed them to process late trades without outside assistance. The danger with these cases is that they could continue on almost indefinitely because having fewer parties involved creates fewer opportunities for detection or whistleblowing.

Standard illegal arrangements in late trading involved three parties: the client, the broker-dealer, and the back room processing firm. This meant that if one group within the chain developed a conscience and reported their wrongdoing or was caught for something else, the other two parties were at risk for discovery. However, if one party is removed from this chain, then the risk of discovery decreases. This was the case with Bear Sterns and CIBC, as described below.

One-Stop Shysters: Bear Sterns

SEC regulators found that executives within the clearing and private-client services divisions allowed hedge fund clients to market time their accounts. It is believed that those clients which Bear Sterns assisted in market timing gave back to Bear Sterns employees in the form of expensive dinners, tickets to sporting events, and spa treatments (Damato & Burns, 4/5/04, R1). This represented a unique situation among broker-dealers involved in late trading and market timing, in that they received extra compensation outside of increased commissions for their part in arranging illegal trades. Because of these extra payments, brokers were not only violating rules regarding trading, they were also in violation of compensation rules, which place limits on the amount of compensation a broker may receive from a client. These rules were put in place to prevent the type of favoritism demonstrated during this scandal, as only certain clients were given access to illegal trading opportunities which reduced investment risk and increased the likelihood of quick trading profits.

In addition to accusations made against brokers at Bear Sterns, there are allegations that Bear Sterns acted as a clearing house for smaller brokers, allowing hedge funds to illegally trade in mutual funds (Goldstein, 11/13/03). This is especially dangerous for the fund industry, because Bear Sterns acted as one of the largest fund clearing houses on Wall Street, meaning that they had the potential to bring tremendous volume to market timing and late trading, in addition to the dangers discussed above of an in-house corrupt clearing house. Both Kaplan Securities and Empire Financial Holdings also used Bear Sterns as a clearing house. The Florida brokerage firms were under regulatory scrutiny and Kaplan was ultimately fined $750k for late trading and market timing. Empire was a small, on-line brokerage firm and had agreements with Canary Capital. Kaplan Securities was also connected with Canary Capital, and was the first firm to enter into a late trading agreement with the hedge fund (SEC, 11/19/03).

According to a lawsuit by regulators, Bear Sterns created and promoted an "electronic routing system" which facilitated market timing and late trading for hedge funds and small brokerage firms. Allegedly, Bear Sterns, "generated substantial revenues and profits from participating in the illegal conduct [by traders] (Goldstein, 11/13/03)". The system allowed Bear Sterns to collect a commission from every mutual fund trade conducted using this platform. This move makes the illegality virtually invisible, as the clearing division conceals it to look like a normal transaction, preventing any regulators who would have normally examined Bear Sterns' records from detecting illegal activities.

One-stop shysters: Canadian Imperial Bank of Commerce

This was the second case of a broker-dealer participating in all facets of the illicit transaction. The Canadian Imperial Bank of Commerce (CIBC) colluded with a hedge fund to conduct illegal trades and then provided the clearinghouse to process the orders, just as Bear Sterns had done. CIBC took their criminality a step further when they funded the offending investors. Regulators allege that CIBC lent over $2 billion to hedge funds so that these investors could market time and late trade, with CIBC also acting as broker and back office in addition to being the banker in the scheme. The scheme is alleged to have continued from 1998 to 2003, resulting in over $75 million in fees earned directly from these loans and services (Goldstein, 12/2/03). By controlling the complete process of illegal trading and minimize the amount of outside forces, organizations like CIBC and Bear Sterns are allowed to maintain all functions of the trading business in-house, reducing oversight on their activities and resulting in easier completion of illegal trades with less risk of being detected.

Cover-Ups

One of the consistent features of this scandal was broker-dealers covering up their illegal trades through various means, benefiting from a lack of transparency and clear rules or regulations regarding a broker-dealer's responsibilities regarding providing customer information to mutual funds. Before new regulations were passed in response to the market timing and late trading scandal, mutual funds were allowed to hold customer's funds in omnibus accounts, which made it difficult for a mutual fund to determine whether or not an investor was market timing. Even if mutual funds chose to enforce their own rules regarding market timing, they had a difficult time identifying market timing investors because the brokers would assist their customers in obscuring the illegal activity. Brokers could break up large trades into smaller trades or spread trades over multiple fictitious accounts, so that the fund companies would be less likely to be alerted. The frequency of this practice is evident from the amount of letters and emails from mutual fund companies to brokers asking them to stop market timing. The fund companies did have the right to block the customer's account from trading, but this is subverted by simply opening a new account in a new name. If a company was blocked, the broker-dealer could use a different company name, which took a little more work, but still occurred. Even those mutual fund companies successfully blocking market timing were only garnering Pyrrhic victories, as blocking a market timer hurt the company's bottom line, creating a conflict of priorities.

This practice of covering up illegal actions by making trades smaller or by using false names and subsidiaries is common to several types and cases of white-collar crime. Calavita, Pontell, and Tillman (1997) found that cover-ups were a common factor among fraudulent savings and loans, as they attempted to doctor their loans to make them look more reasonable to regulators during their routine examinations. A U.S. Government Accountability Office study cited by the researchers noted that in a sample of 179 violations of criminal fraud 42 of those were related to cover-up activities, making it the largest single crime category (Calavita, Pontell, & Tillman, 1997, p. 65). Studies on accounting frauds from the early 2000's found that several companies used subsidiaries strictly for the purpose of hiding their losses from bad deals. Enron famously exploited this accounting loophole to hide billions in losses in fake subsidiaries which had been given Star Wars related names by science fiction fan and Enron CFO Andrew Fastow (McLean & Elkind, 2003).

Cover-Ups: Canadian Imperial Bank of Commerce

Over the five years that CIBC operated these schemes they received over one thousand letters and emails from mutual fund companies complaining about one of their broker's, Michael Sassano's, trading practices. This is a tremendous amount of mail to receive over the actions of a few brokers, which indicates that CIBC must have had knowledge that some of their brokers were participating in illegal trading schemes. Regulators allege that rather than restrict Sassano and his team, the group was given permission to use deceptive practices to hide their abusive trading, including: using multiple accounts to hide the trades' origins, creating corporate subsidiaries to hide CIBC's involvement, and establishing accounts through Fidelity Investments and Charles Schwab to gain access to mutual funds they offered and further cover their tracks. (Goldstein, 12/2/03).

Cover-Ups: Bear Sterns

During the years of abusive trading practices Bear Sterns received thousands of complaints from mutual fund companies about late trading in their funds. However, Bear Sterns did not desist until the fund company threatened to terminate dealer agreements between the two companies (Damato & Burns, 4/5/04). This is an example of how much abuse a fund had to tolerate when a company the size of Bear Sterns was involved in illegal schemes. Mutual fund companies still tried to complain to Bear Sterns for years, even after it must have been obvious that the company was not going to stop its illegal and abusive trading practices.

Cover-Ups: Prudential

Like the other companies, Prudential received complaints from mutual funds, but it was on a larger scale. Regulators found more than 25,000 from sixty-eight different mutual fund companies covering a twelve month period, asking that Prudential stop abusive trading practices (Henriques, 12/11/03). As in other cases, brokers from Prudential tried to avoid detection by creating new accounts from which to trade and splitting trades into multiple smaller trades in attempt to avoid detection. This was the most egregious case of market timing, as evidenced both by the number of emails that Prudential received (an average of over one email per day, per mutual fund company, for a year) and the large fine that Prudential received. It was the largest fine for any organization penalized during the mutual fund scandal, $330 million in fines alone.

Corporate Culture and Learning

Another feature of the mutual fund scandal that was present among multiple broker-dealers was how illegalities seemed to generally involve only a few members of the organization who were all on the same team or unit. In addition, there was even a case of three brokers who were all involved in market timing while at separate companies, having worked together early in their careers. This is a common refrain when politicians and lawmakers discuss corporate crime, as they blame "a few bad apples" (Meyer, 6/26/02). However, the full saying is that "A few bad apples, spoils the bushel". This saying is more apropos in describing the way that corrupt culture is learned and adopted by employees within an organization. This section will briefly examine cases of concentrated corruption within the organization with references to its relevance in white-collar crime study.

Evidence about management's role in the scandal also supports previous white-collar crime scholarship. Jenkins and Braithwaite (1993) found pressure for the worst types of corporate crime coming from the organization's management and filtering down to employees. Interview research with company executives demonstrates a relationship between top management's attitudes and the level of that corporation's compliance with the law (Clinard, 1983). Data on compliance with nursing home regulations confirmed that when pressure for profits is greatest, the boss is most likely to say, "This is the bottom line that I want. I don't care (and I don't want to know) what you have to do to get there (Jenkins & Braithwaite, 1993, p. 230)." Geis found that offenders in the heavy electrical equipment antitrust cases were introduced to price-fixing practices by their bosses (Geis, 1967). This indicates that management can motivate their employees to engage in crime by creating a company attitude that condones crime, pushing employees for results regardless of the means, and/or directly introducing employees to illegal practices.

Corporate Culture and Learning: Prudential

The case against Prudential is centered on four brokers in the institution's New York offices – Skifter Ajro, Fredrick O'Meally, Robert Shannon, and team leader Martin Druffner – who concocted an elaborate plan to execute up to a thousand trades a day for their hedge fund clients by disguising the trades' origins (Goldstein, 08/02/05). This alone should have alerted company officials and regulators, because that many trades from a single broker should probably a red flag. However, this practice continued uninterrupted by Prudential management.

Prudential eventually fired the four brokers, as the mutual fund investigations were announced. The brokers contend that, during their time with Prudential, their practices were accepted and open. Mr. O'Meally, one of the fired brokers, said, "No one told me to change anything and no one said I was doing anything wrong." He believes that Prudential "threw the brokers under the bus hoping to minimize the involvement of the company and portray them as rogue brokers" (Rosen, 11/17/06). However, it is noticeable that no other Prudential brokers were ever mentioned or sanctioned as a result of Spitzer's investigations into the company. The tremendous pressure to succeed often creates a game of "follow the leader" among the financial community. If O'Meally and the three other brokers were acting in a legal, successful manner, they would have had many other copycats within the company.

In July 2011, Druffner and Ajro were found gulity in a federal civil case and ordered to pay a total of $1,255,584 in disgorgement and prejudgement interest (SEC, 7/18/11). The SEC brought civil cases against both former Prudential employees for their knowledge of market timing practices despited mutual fund companies active prohibition of such activities. A jury found O'Meally guilty of six counts of negligence in his dealings with mutual funds (SEC, 12/16/11).

Corporate Culture and Learning: CIBC

Spitzer alleged that CIBC Oppenheimer broker Michael Sassano and his ten employee team of brokers regularly engaged in market timing and late trading. There is evidence that Sassano and his team were the only brokers at CIBC Oppenheimer who were allowed to engage in these types of activities and it is estimated that they earned $40 million in commissions from 1998 to 2002 while engaging in this form of abusive mutual fund trading for hedge funds. Sassano's success from market timing and late trading earned him several promotions while at Oppenheimer. He eventually became a "managing director" and had an office on the same floor as senior executives, rather than with his team or other managers.

It is alleged that Sassano and Flynn (the CIBC trader who had criminal charges brought against him by Eliot Spitzer) actively worked together, with Sasssano recruiting the hedge funds and then passing them along to Flynn so that he could create financing them to engage in their abusive trading strategies. This partnership also allowed hedge funds to evade normal regulations regarding trading with borrowed money (Goldstein, 7/20/05). Flynn even provided financing for Sassano to form his own hedge fund, Atlantique Capital Advisors, which was created specifically to engage in market timing. This is known because Massachusetts regulators have charged AG Edwards' Boston office with using deceptive techniques to hide market timing practices for several hedge funds, including Atlantique-AG Edwards ultimately settled the charges for almost $4 million in fines and restitution (Goldstein, 7/20/05).

Corporate Learning: the CIBC/Prudential/Bank of America Nexus

Ironically, Sassano was formerly employed at Lehman Brothers in the mid-1990's with three other central figures in the mutual fund scandal, Theodore Sihpol, Martin Druffner and Frederick O'Meally. Druffner and O'Meally, who were discussed in the above section on Prudential, were alleged to have been good friends with Sassano. Sihpol also worked at CIBC World Markets for two years while Sassano was working there (Goldstein, 12/02/03). It is not known whether Lehman Brothers is or was actively engaged in market timing, but it is quite a coincidence that four brokers who all worked together at the same institution are all later sanctioned for committing the same act at different organizations.

Effects on Mutual Funds After They Were Sanctioned

Some offending mutual funds received negative responses from investors in the form of large-scale withdrawals of their investments. This reaction by investors was to be expected by many of the business community. In fact, it is part of the theory posited by neo-conservative economists on why white-collar crime is not a problem. They suppose that a free-market context allows customers to regulate the industry with their dollars, enabling investors to move their assets from companies committing illegal acts and harming the investors to those companies that do not commit illegal acts. The theory then posits that companies will avoid illegal acts because they do not want to damage their reputations and lose business as customers discover illegalities and move their money to more honest firms (Easterbrook & Fischel, 1991). Despite the theory's common sense nature, the reality of the mutual fund scandal, and other white-collar offenses, does not support this neo-conservative hypothetical. All but one of the companies involved in the scandal still exist (and the one was forced closed by government regulators), so market timing and late trading did not drive away all of their respective customers. Also, some offending companies did not lose any significant business after the scandal. This either suggests that the theory is incorrect or customers remained uninformed of the state of their investments. Regardless, this evidence runs contrary to the theory inasmuch, as perfect knowledge by the customer is assumed; the case studies show clearly that this is simply not the case.

While neo-conservative economic theories of regulation do not receive empirical support, theories from other disciplines share some common elements. Publicity is a component of the complete consumer knowledge aspect of neo-conservative economic theory, and this aspect is present in other theories of regulation. Legal and media figures have advocated the positive societal effect of publicity as a regulatory agent. Former Supreme Court Justice Louis Brandeis wrote in a 1913 Harper's Weekly article that, "Sunlight is said to be the best of disinfectants;

electric light the most efficient policeman (Brandeis, 12/20/13)." Famed politician and media mogul Joseph Pulitzer commented,

> There is not a crime, there is not a dodge, there is not a trick, there is not a swindle, there is not a vice which does not live by secrecy. Get these things out in the open, describe them, attack them, ridicule them in the press, and sooner or later public opinion will sweep them away. Publicity may not be the only thing that is needed, but it is the only thing without which all other agencies fail (Boulton, 1978, p. 253).

It is the exposure to light that many theorists propose as an effective deterrent to white-collar crime.

Fisse and Braithwaite have done empirical research on the effect of publicity on corporate offenders. They conducted interviews at seventeen large, transnational corporations that suffered adverse publicity since the 1960's as a result of gross misbehavior that was either criminal at the time or criminalized as a result of that case. However, the scholars found that those cases which did not directly affect customers had little to no effect on sales, while cases affecting customers had a substantial, negative impact on sales; and only a small minority of cases had any negative financial impact on the offending company (Fisse & Braithwaite, 1983, p. 229, 243). In the case of mutual funds, there were reports of a negative financial impact for some fund companies, which is to be expected given market timing and late trading directly affected customers' bottom lines. However, it is surprising that some offending companies did not suffer a negative impact from their involvement in the late trading and/or market timing scandal. In fact, some of these companies actually showed positive results in the year following their settlement (Houge & Wellman, 2005, p. 133).

Timing of the settlement may have had a larger effect on its impact, rather than the fact that a company was involved in the scandal at all. This issue ties into a later discussion of how punishments changed over time, but it seems that companies punished first were more likely to face negative impacts than companies punished later. The three cases discussed below (Alliance Capital, Janus, and Putnam) were all settled within twelve months of the Canary Capital case being settled, which denoted the beginning of market timing and late trading scandal and its notoriety in the media.

This measure of customer reaction is complicated because it is difficult to quantify mutual funds' losses over this time period for two reasons. One, mutual funds do not publish how many customers they have or how many have divested from the mutual fund. Unless a fund company is willing to share that information, the only reasonable metric is the fund's value. However, this figure is also difficult to parse out because the stock market affects a fund's value as well. Mutual funds could lose money because of their investments, even if they did not lose customers due to negative publicity. This complex metric relates to difficulties in distinguishing the relationship between the settlements timing and the amount of publicity that a story receives. It is logical that the first settlements received the most notoriety, as new stories tend to receive more attention than older stories-and this scandal continued approximately five years, with the last settlements occurring in the summer of 2008. So, the real factor in losing customers may be related to a new story's prominence, rather than when a settlement occurred. In fact, there are studies that an upward market results in investors focusing on positive news and filtering out negative news, while the opposite occurs in a down market. Hersh M. Sefrin, described the phenomenon as such, "It takes a down market to generate traction, when investors have a very strong need to feel that what's happened is not their fault. That's when the issues involving impropriety gain traction" (McGeehan, 1/11/04).

Effects on Mutual Funds After They Were Sanctioned: Putnam

The largest retirement system in America, California Public Employees Retirement System (CalPERS), announced, soon after the settlement, they had fired Putnam Investments as manager of their $1.2 billion stock investment account. CalPERS President Sean Harrigan said, "Putnam's former senior management breached their general fiduciary duty by failing to act when their compliance office first reported improper trading activities (Shinal, 11/18/03)." Massachusetts, Iowa, and New York state pension funds also voted to remove their accounts from Putnam. Within months after the settlement, approximately $60 billion-25%-of Putnam's assets had been removed by investors (Houge & Wellman, 2005, p. 133).

Company CEO's have admitted that some of Putnam's financial struggles after news of their involvement were due to "reputational problems". However, they also noted that investors care less about legal problems than results and performance (Levitz, 2/27/06). This contradicts economic theory, but could be an explanation for why some mutual funds did not suffer investor backlash. This is substantiated by a *Wall Street Journal* article which noted that while Putnam suffered large divestments, other companies such as MFS-who was fined more than twice as much as Putnam for their involvement in the scandal-continued "relatively unscathed". The article stated that MFS owed their ability to continue and succeed due to the fund company's performance (Johannes, 1/24/05).

Effects on Mutual Funds After They Were Sanctioned: Janus

Soon after Janus settled charges of negotiated market timing with the SEC and New York and Colorado State Attorney Generals' offices; ING Financial Services announced that they would be withdrawing $5 billion in investments from Janus. This is estimated to be about 4% of Janus' total assets at the time of the announcement (MSNBC, 8/18/04). It is also estimated that investors withdrew a total of $28.5 billion within the nine months since the scandal emerged (Greenberg, 7/22/04). This is a significant loss for Janus, in terms of investments. However, the irony of the situation is that less than one year later, ING Financial Services was penalized a total of almost $3 million dollars for negotiated market timing (Weber, 9/6/04). Janus settled their case eleven months after the scandal began, after fifteen other companies had already negotiated settlements. They also received a relatively large penalty ($226 million), but were only the eighth most punished organization. Despite this, Janus received some of the harshest investor backlash among involved companies. However, among companies punished relatively strongly and early, Janus may have been the most prominent name. It is possible that this combination of factors contributed to the amount of divestment.

Effects on Mutual Funds After They Were Sanctioned: Alliance Capital

Unlike other funds involved in the mutual fund scandal, Alliance did not suffer a mass exodus of investors. This has baffled some mutual fund experts, although, they claim, there are some reasons for the difference in outcomes. Dan Culloton, a mutual fund analyst at Morningstar said, "[Alliance Capital] probably hasn't suffered much in terms of redemptions because their funds are broker-sold. Also, there are more spectacular cases of market-timing, like at Putnam

Investments (Gilpin, 11/2/03)." Adding to its low profile, the firm merged with a stock research and money management firm, Bernstein & Company, in 2001. The corporation has since become known as Alliance Bernstein and the Bernstein side of the company has taken over more management controls since the mutual fund scandal, which may have mitigated negative perceptions from investors. Alliance also did not have the prominent name of a Janus or Putnam, which, like MFS Investments, may have allowed them to avoid large investor withdrawals.

Common and Uncommon Punishments

Among those organizations most severely punished, there are few apparent commonalities. One factor that does stand out is large fee reductions included among their sanctions. This is true for seven of the top ten most penalized, and there were no fee reductions for any organization that fell below the median punishment of $20,000,000. Logically, including large fee reductions increased the total punishment, pushing that organization higher up the list. However, only Spitzer enforced fee reductions as part of a punishment, so Spitzer was commonly involved in negotiating settlements with the most heavily punished organizations. In fact, Spitzer was only involved in one case that resulted in a punishment below the median.

The mean punishment for organizations involved in market timing and/or late trading was $89,507,025, a figure skewed by each of the top three punishments being almost double that of the fourth largest punishment (refer to Appendix 3). Nonetheless, nineteen organizations received punishments above the mean. Spitzer was involved in fifteen of those cases. Of the bottom twenty-two cases, the NASD/FINRA was the sole regulatory body for twenty of them, with fourteen settlements under $1 million dollars. These groups represent opposites in terms of their jurisdictional boundaries and goals. Because of the Martin Law, Spitzer, essentially, eliminated his jurisdictional restraints and focused on large cases that would make headlines and send a message. The NASD/FINRA is bounded, as an SRO, to adjudicating broker-dealers only, and would be alone in those cases that the SEC deemed too insignificant to join in the investigation and settlement.

Of course, these numbers represent only those that were punished by either a self-regulatory organization, or a state or federal regulatory body. Data on individual investors' illegal activity is not available because no individuals were sanctioned, outside of fiduciaries or executives for investment companies. This is not to say that mutual fund companies did not ban or restrict individual investors that were caught performing illegal trades. However, data on these illegal activities is not publicly available, nor does it involve financial penalties or possible incarceration.

Trends of Penalties over Time

Calavita and Pontell's analysis of the savings and loan prosecutions found that aggressive punishment of "thrift" offenders diminished over time. The government's response to S&Ls shifted with the involvement of political actors whose careers were closely tied to thrift lobbyists. The government's response changed from "crime control" to "damage control" (Calavita & Pontell, 1995). Similar to the Savings and Loan scandal, several of the same mutual funds involved in the late trading and market timing scandal have been active in politics through campaign donations and other ties to political figures. The first issue broached here will be the treatment of those actors and organizations who were both politically active as well as being involved in the market timing and late trading scandal. Then this section will seek to discover any punishment trends over the scandal's timeline.

Smith Barney and UBS AG fired brokers after their own internal investigations discovered misconduct. They then managed to avoid any sanctions from federal regulators, but were each penalized over $50 million dollars each from a partnership of New Jersey's state attorney general and the self-regulatory arm of the New York Stock Exchange, which were the only two cases this partnership punished by themselves. UBS AG's employees and political action committees gave over $470,000 to George W. Bush's 2004 Presidential campaign (Center for Responsive Politics, 4/16/08). Smith Barney is owned by Citigroup, and Citigroup gave approximately $320,000 through their employees and political action committees. However, UBS, Smith Barney, and Bush had a relationship stemming back to Bush's tenure at Harken Energy Corporation. When Harken needed money, Bush and other Harken officials met with Jackson Stephens, a long-time Republican booster who had given $200,000 to the Reagan-Bush and Bush-Quayle campaigns (Lombardi, 1999). Stephens helped arrange a $25 million dollar loan from UBS in return for a stock interest in Harken.

Merril Lynch became involved in the scandal when their internal investigation revealed that their brokers were conducting "improper fund trading." Merril Lynch was never formally charged by any regulatory parties investigating the fund scandal, but they fired some of their brokers. Merril Lynch was also the third largest contributor to the Bush 2004 re-election campaign, donating over $580,000 from employees and political action committees (Center for Responsive Politics, 4/16/08). Ten of the largest twenty contributors to the Bush re-election campaign were investment companies, and seven of those ten displayed some level of involvement in the scandal (Bank of America, UBS AG, Citigroup, Bear Sterns, Morgan Stanley, JP Morgan, and Merril Lynch). Of those seven companies, only three faced financial penalties from the mutual fund scandal (Bank of America, UBS AG, and Bear Sterns), and only one of those was sanctioned by a federal agency (Bank of America).

This relationship between offenders and politicians, while it may show trends of favoritism on a micro scale, is not meant to imply causality between campaign contributions and leniency in white-collar crime settlements. As noted by Bill Maurer such attempts at review are not meant to give a complete picture (Maurer, 2005). Lombardi's artistic rendition of social network connections between former President George W. Bush, Stephens Jackson, UBS, and various oil barons, as well as his pictures of Savings and Loan social networks, are mere reviews of past transactions rather than proof of continuing collusion or established relationships of favor or gift exchange. Barring further evidence, they should be taken on face value, as demonstrating past exchanges and current situations and circumstances. In this case, there was a past relationship wherein UBS aided George W. Bush and his colleagues when Bush's business was in financial trouble. Many years later, Bush was President and UBS contributed hundreds of thousands of dollars to his campaign. It should also be noted that they contributed hundreds of thousands to other successful and failed Presidential campaigns within the last two election cycles (Center for Responsive Politics, 4/16/08). During Bush's presidency UBS was investigated as part of the market timing and late trading scandal. No federal agencies brought charges against the organization, but the New Jersey Attorney General's office and the self-regulatory division of the New York Stock Exchange reached a settlement with UBS. They found that UBS attempted to hide their brokers' market timing activities, and did not implement an effective system of internal controls to prevent market timing in the first place (Stempel, 6/11/08). They penalized UBS over $32 million in fines, as well as $18 million in disgorgement of their illicit profits. This is may suggest impropriety, or at least failure by regulatory organizations, but it does not demonstrate political favoritism or bias in the handling of the UBS case. Even incorporating Pontell and Calavita's state theory that prosecutions decreased over time with the involvement of politically connected figures, connections between Bush and UBS could be coincidence. There are many variables involved in the process of investigating cases and punishing offenders, and it would be difficult to definitively state what happened in these two instances. It is best to describe it as a past relationship, take note of the coincidence, and move forward with the discussion, all the while keeping this relationship in mind in case other, similar instances emerge.

In Calavita and Pontell's study of the Savings and Loan scandal they noticed a trend of diminishing punishments over time, where the first offenders to be tried or settle their cases received harsher penalties than later cases (Calavita & Pontell, 1994). They attributed this trend to state theories of punishment, in which cases went from deterrence to management and protection of politically important actors that were involved in the illegal activities.

In this scandal, trends of decreasing punishment are not as discernible. This may come from the simple fact that there were fewer cases (sixty-two as opposed to the hundreds of cases in the Savings and Loan scandal). In addition, more cases were handled by regulatory agencies or state agencies, and with fewer criminal cases. This allowed for more consistent punishment, as a formula for fines and disgorgement had been created by the SEC, and federal oversight required that this formula be applied consistently. In support of this notion, the greatest cause of variation in penalties applied came from Spitzer's requirement of fee reductions. This was one area that was completely outside the standard punishment formula and did not involve regulatory agencies at all. In fact, the regulatory agencies publicly disapproved of including fee reductions in the settlements (SEC, 12/18/03).

Differences between punishments from agencies are discernible through use of a scatter plot graph (see Appendix 5). From this graph it is obvious that the cases involving Eliot Spitzer and the New York Attorney General's office generally received harsher penalties than those cases in which he was not involved. It should be noted that every case which featured Eliot Spitzer's office also included the SEC, except in the Canary Capital case – the initial case of the mutual fund scandal – which Spitzer's office handled alone. Other state and federal agencies were sometimes involved with Eliot Spitzer, but the SEC was the only consistent entity. There were a few cases in which the NASD/FINRA worked in collaboration with other agencies; however, the majority of their cases were handled alone. As previously mentioned, the NASD/FINRA cases were generally smaller and focused on broker-dealers. Again, demonstrating an effective use of the Legal-Pluralist model of regulation (Braithwaite, 1995), allowing a type of specialization in pursuing offender sanctioning. This is borne out by examining cases handled exclusively by the NASD/FINRA. In twenty of the twenty-two "smallest" cases-in terms of total penalty issued- the NASD/FINRA worked alone (see Appendix 3).

If cases involving Eliot Spitzer's office received the largest penalties, then SEC cases were the second largest. However, this is more complex than it appears due to the amount of collaboration in prosecuting these cases. Multiple agencies prosecuted all but nine of the forty-one cases not involving the NASD/FINRA which resulted in financial sanctions. Of the nine solo cases, the SEC prosecuted eight of them, and the ninth case was the Canary Capital case, handled by the New York State Attorney General's office. Seven of the eight cases handled by the SEC alone came in well under the mean punishment, with fines and disgorgements ranging from $50 million to just under $3.5 million. However, they did have one case, against Security Brokerage, Inc., which resulted in total penalties over $150 million. Due to the SEC's penalty formula being applied in these cases, it appears as though sanctions in these cases hinged on the amount of offenses that took place and the offender's illicit profit.

Due to the limited number of cases that comprise the market timing and late trading scandal, possible effects or trends are magnified by dividing this population of cases into sample populations based upon who prosecuted the case. Nonetheless, the group does divide fairly evenly with twenty cases attributable to Spitzer, nineteen to the SEC, and twenty-one to the NASD/FINRA. The Spitzer case penalties averaged $185,077,250; the SEC cases averaged $50,828,053; and the NASD/FINRA averaged $1,393,175. As mentioned above, some of these discrepancies are associated with fee reductions which Spitzer imposed in almost all of his cases. The difference in the SEC and

NASD penalties likely reflect the jurisdictional and resource differences also discussed above.

While mean sanctions are informative in comparing the quantity of monetary punishment inflicted by various agencies and organizations, another valuable statistic is the regression line for these cases (see Appendices 5 and 6). This gives an indication of the average case settlements over time-the unit of analysis for Pontell and Calavita. In this study, Spitzer's settlements show a relatively steep decline over time – $5,346,768 for every month after the initial Canary Capital case was settled in September 2003. This statistic is interesting, although a bit deceiving, as the initial Canary Capital case represented a $40 million settlement, followed by a $600 million settlement three months later, followed by $540 million and $140 million settlements six months after the initial case. Nonetheless, Spitzer's twenty cases did demonstrate this steep decline.

SEC cases also showed a much more gradual decline, with a negative slope of $381,238 dollars for every month after the initial settlement. This statistic comes with caveats as well. In the SEC's case, they were not even aware of investigations into market timing and late trading when Spitzer made his announcement of the settlement with Canary Capital. Their first market timing and late trading settlement did not come until March 2004, six months after the Canary settlement-which impacts the calculation of their regression line. The NASD/FINRA settlements have the same disadvantageous late start in prosecuting market timing and late trading cases. Despite this, their slope maintained a slightly positive bent, increasing an average of $46,686 per month after the Canary settlement. However, it should be noted that even with a slightly positive slope over the 21 cases, the range of NASD/FINRA settlements was much smaller relative to that of the SEC or Spitzer cases, with the highest settlement being $5 million and the lowest $100,000. The Spitzer cases ranged from $600 million to $4.2 million, while the SEC cases varied between $250 million and $350,000.

These results add a nuance to Pontell and Calavita's (1995) findings that penalties decreased over time as a result of defendants being politically involved or connected. In these cases politically connected defendants were punished for their involvement. The difference in this scandal is that even though there was punishment, there was also a show of leniency or bias, as federal-level regulators did not sanction the politically connected offenders. Instead, these offenders were penalized by self-regulatory organizations and state regulatory agencies, or they sanctioned themselves by firing employees. This demonstrates a possible form of bias as described by Goetz (1997) in his research on arson-for-profit viewed as white-collar crime. As Goetz explains, there are multiple forms of bias which are exercised by powerful members of the criminal justice system that may represent leniency to certain members or classes of defendants. The traditional form is commonly understood, and it is represented in white-collar crime cases through lesser sentences for white-collar crimes versus non-white-collar crimes. The second and third forms of bias are less commonly understood and they are expressed through treatment of the offender outside of traditional sanctions. In this case, as in Goetz's example of arsonists, we observe bias by not allowing the offense to be labeled "crime" so that an offender is not considered to be a criminal. This was demonstrated in market timing and late trading cases when federal agencies did not push for formal charges against UBS and Merril Lynch. Although it is difficult to know how much bias was expressed in the Merill Lynch case, as no agency pushed for formal sanctions, the UBS case is quantifiable because state and self-regulatory organizations issued a total penalty of $50,500,000 and UBS fired two people. Federal regulators, by choosing not to elevate their investigation into charges, would not have attached an "offender" label. The Merrill case is more ambiguous as all sanctions were self-imposed, so except for a few one line mentions in news reports no offender label was attached to them through any regulatory agencies or media outlets.

Determining Sanctions

The Government Accountability Office (GAO) report "Challenges Remain," three primary criteria the SEC used to determine penalties levied against organizations and individuals: profit made by the organization or individual, cooperation from the offender in settling the case, and type of offenses involved (GAO, 2005c). Other secondary criteria were also considered, but these were the most consistent across all cases. In this section, the SEC penalties will be examined to understand how profit and cooperation affected penalties at the micro-level.

As mentioned above, the "challenges remain" report highlights findings that the SEC obtained from those mutual fund cases settled up until that report was published. The SEC had imposed fourteen actions against mutual fund companies and ten actions against other types of firms (GAO, 2005c). The GAO found that the SEC used a formula in determining penalties that was consistent with other cases against investment advisers and corporate accounting frauds. They also found that the SEC coordinated penalties and disgorgement with state authorities, although some states obtained additional penalties to what the SEC negotiated.

The SEC also included a number of additional factors to affect the amount of penalty they imposed (egregiousness of conduct, degree of harm to investors, extent of defendant's cooperation, economic benefit gained by the defendant, duration of the conduct, size of the firm, defendant's recidivism, need for deterrence, and the defendant's ability of pay) (GAO, 2005b). Spokespersons from the SEC said that relatively high penalties in market timing and late trading cases were imposed to increase accountability and enhance deterrence in the securities industry (GAO, 2005b). However, the SEC did not always follow maximum penalty guidelines, as listed above.

While the settlements reached by mutual fund companies were not trivial, the Securities Enforcement Remedies and Penny Stock Reform Act of 1990's tiered system, plus the large number of violations involved in each case would have resulted in astronomical fines. The SEC sought lower penalties in many cases; because they believed there was minimal financial damage from these crimes, and they worried that high penalties would have decreased chances of reaching settlements (GAO, 2005b).

Leniency for Offenders?

Shapiro has argued that the utilization of alternative sanctions such as civil remedies in response to white-collar offenses need to be considered by enforcers. She argues "any apparent discrimination against lower status offenders in prosecutorial discretion is more readily explained by greater access to legal options than by social standing (Shapiro, 1990, pp. 361-362)." Although these two factors are likely related, she calls for a re-conceptualization of the white-collar leniency thesis, in that "arguments that attribute leniency accorded to white-collar offenders to class bias misunderstand the structural sources of leniency." However, research has found that fining individuals and companies for their offenses is a rather weak sanction. In his seminal study of the heavy electrical equipment anti-trust cases from the 1960s,

Gilbert Geis noted that a $400,000 fine against General Electric was the financial equivalent of a person earning $175,000 a year receiving a $3 parking ticket (Geis, 1967). Likewise, in the mutual fund scandal, Bank of America received the largest total penalty at $685 million, yet they still earned $14.1 billion in 2004, making them the world's fifth most profitable company (Bank of America Annual Report, 2004). Prudential, who received the second largest total penalty at $600 million, earned $3.14 billion in 2006-the year they were punished. (Prudential Annual Report, 2006). This represented less than 5% of Bank of America's earnings and less than 20% of Prudential's earnings, although the actual figure may be less as penalties may be factored into the respective earnings' figures. These earning's figures are deceptive, as they are commonly thought of as a company's income. However, earnings are really a company's profit, or, to put it in personal terms, savings.

It should also be noted that while the total penalty in each of the aforementioned cases looks daunting, it is actually comprised of smaller numbers that diminish the penalty's impact. For example, Bear Sterns received a $250 million penalty. Of that $250 million $160 million was restitution with interest, meaning that regulators were simply removing illegal profits that the firm had already received. This is less of a penalty, than simply righting a wrong. Not to mention that these numbers come only from those infractions that are uncovered and can be proven. Considering how little white-collar crime actually gets discovered it is naïve to think that when an ongoing, widespread infraction is discovered, that regulators are able to accurately identify the total amount of damage done. In Bear Sterns' case, this left a $90 million dollar penalty. Bear Sterns' made over $500 million in the first quarter of 2006 (the year the fine was imposed). This means that for four years of stealing from customers they were forced to return some percentage of their illicit profits and then penalized less than 20% of their profits from the first three months of 2006. If one were to put this in terms of income, Bear Sterns earned $3.6 billion in the first quarter of 2006, which means the fine was approximately one-fifteenth of their first quarter income (Weiss, 3/25/06). To use a metaphor like Geis used in 1967, would you risk robbing a bank if your penalty would be to return as much of the money as the government could determine you stole, plus pay a fine equivalent to six days worth of your salary? You also would not be required to admit to doing anything wrong or face any further sanction. As a reference point, the average federal sentence for robbery in fiscal year 2010 was 76.8 months (USSC, 2010).

Penalty Differentials Based upon Case Characteristics

The majority of companies caught market timing, late trading, or facilitating these behaviors on behalf of others, entered into plea agreements. Their punishments, ostensibly, required them to pay back the monies gained from illegal activities. Many involved employees were also fired and received some length of suspension from the securities industry. These bans ranged from 23 days to a lifetime, although one year was the modal ban period (GAO, 2005b). The following are brief case summaries that demonstrate how the varied nature of cases was reflected in the punishments that they received.

Canary Capital

Canary Capital Partners represents a unique case within the mutual fund scandal. It was the original case, and Eddie Stern and his partners were given special consideration for their cooperation in uncovering illegal arrangements throughout the industry, which directly resulted in at least six settlements with other organizations. This leverage would not have been available for offenders discovered later in the process, and may explain the lack of criminal prosecution and relatively light penalty against Stern and his associates, given their offenses. The $40 million fine levied in the Canary Capital case was determined from estimates that Stern had received approximately $40 million in Canary management and incentive fees during the time that he was conducting his illegal trading practices (Brown, New York Supreme Court Complaint).

Bank of America

Other companies were actively involved in soliciting, promoting, and conducting illegal trades through their trading platforms. In March 2004, Bank of America paid a $375 million dollar penalty, which included $125 million in fines and $250 million in restitution for investors. At this time, Bank of America was purchasing FleetBoston Bank, which was also accused of participating in the mutual fund scandal. Spitzer and the SEC allege that FleetBoston's Columbia funds allowed traders to make $2.5 billion worth of market timing trades in seven different mutual funds between 1998 and the summer of 2003. FleetBoston agreed to pay $70 million in fines and $70 million in restitution in conjunction with the Bank of America settlement. The two merging banks also agreed to reduce their fees by a combined $160 million over the next five years (Beltran, 3/15/04). Together, the two banks paid the largest penalty of any organization involved in the mutual fund scandal.

In addition to the suits against the company, Bank of America fired executive Charles Bryceland, mutual fund chief Robert Gordon, and broker Theodore Sihpol III for their involvement in the mutual fund scandal. Bank of America also dismissed eight members from their board of directors. Spitzer said about these dismissals, "These directors clearly failed to protect the interest of investors. They acknowledged the problem of market timing, but then allowed a favored client to engage in that harmful practice. The departure of these board members should sound an alarm for all those who serve in similar capacities" (MSNBC, 3/15/04). In all, Bank of America fired a total of ten employees, the third most employees fired by any organization implicated in the scandal.

Alliance Capital Management

Among mutual fund companies caught in the market timing and late trading scandal, Alliance Capital Management incurred the largest penalty. Bank of America received a $685 million penalty and Prudential received a $600 million penalty, but both organizations are brokerage firms who either took advantage of lax or complicit mutual fund companies and/or participated in self-dealings where they pilfered from mutual funds run by their respective companies. Alliance was exclusively a mutual fund company that faced severe punishment for allowing market timing to persist at their institution. Invesco Funds Group, the next most penalized fund company received approximately half of Alliance Capital's penalty. While the fine and disgorgement were not insignificant ($100 million and $150 million, respectively), the bulk of Alliance Capital's penalty came from the $350 million in estimated five-year fee reductions Eliot Spitzer imposed as part of the plea agreement. This was more than double the next largest fee reduction (Bank of America's $160 million), and prompted this statement from the SEC. "This is a case about illegal market timing, not fees. Therefore, we see no legitimate basis for the Commission to act as a 'rate-setter' and determine how much mutual fund customers should pay for the services they receive in the future from Alliance Capital" (SEC, 12/18/03).

In response to investigations by the SEC and Spitzer, Alliance dismissed two of their executives and replaced them with lower level employees from within the company. Alliance forced out their President and COO, John Carifa, and their chairman of the mutual fund distribution unit, Michael Laughlin (Gilpin, 11/2/03). These two executives were selected because they had oversight responsibilities for the mutual fund business, which allowed, "inappropriate market-timing transactions, some of which had an adverse impact on mutual fund shareholders," Lewis A. Sanders, chief executive of Alliance, said in a statement to the press (Gilpin, 11/2/03). Firing of mutual fund management was a consistent trend as settlements were reached. While these may have been moves to appease investors and regulators, they also symbolize the influence company managers exert upon corporate culture and practices.

Janus

In April 2004 Janus, one of the largest mutual fund families, reached a $225 million settlement to end charges related to the mutual fund scandal. Included in the $225 million was $50 million in fines, $50 million in shareholder restitution, and $125 million in fee reductions over a five year period. The Denver-based Janus corporation also paid an additional $1 million to the Colorado attorney general's office, which was put towards investor education and future enforcement measures (MSNBC, 4/27/04). Spitzer and Colorado Attorney General Ken Salazar jointly announced the settlement, although Spitzer did not appear to have an active role in this investigation which did include the SEC. Days before the settlement was reached, CEO Mark Whiston resigned from the company, even though he had spent less than two years as the head of Janus. Despite this timing, Janus denied that Whiston's resignation had anything to do with the mutual fund scandal (MSNBC, 4/27/04). Janus's fine paid directly to a state government illustrates another common punishment element from this scandal. In fact, this occurred in several other cases (Hartford, Deutsche Bank, Waddell & Reed, UBS AG, AIM Advisors, Ameriprise Financial, and MFS Investments).

In addition to paying fines to state attorney generals, this case also contained an egregious element not found in other cases. Janus acknowledged having ten written market timing agreements with different hedge funds (although the SEC alleges that there were at least twelve such agreements), including two accounts that were never funded. Janus also admitted to earning $31.5 million from these arrangements. The SEC administrative court found that two former Janus executives, Warren Lammert and Lars Soderberg, allowed market timing to take place at their company (SEC, 5/29/08). Warren Lammert was manager of Janus' Mercury fund from 1993 to 2003, and Lars Soderberg was executive vice-president and managing director of institutional services from 2003 to 2004 (USAToday.com, 8/2/06). An excerpt from a Janus Capital Group (JCG) email was released regarding how market timing was viewed internally:

> As discussed today, here is a draft of our parameters which we would use sparingly, on an exception only basis, to allow limited timing activity. Our stated policy is that we do not tolerate timers. As such, we won't actively seek timers, but when pressed and when we believe allowing a limited/controlled amount of timing activity will be in JCG's best interests (increased profitability to the firm) we will make exceptions under those parameters (Goldstein, 8/28/06).

These emails show the level of complicity that occurred within mutual fund companies such as Janus, as they clearly approved the violation of their own rules in search of added profits. The most alarming factor may be how Janus and others abused their position for relatively little financial gain. Analyses carried out by Johnathan Burton from CBS Market Watch suggests that Janus earned approximately $5 million a year from market timing, while earning a net profit of $300 million in 2001 alone (Burton, 9/18/03). This may have been a larger factor in down years at the company, but still represents a minor percentage of potential income. This fact illustrates the extreme actions that the management of financial firms will undertake to maximize profit in the short-term while risking the long-term reputation of their organization.

Bear Sterns

On December 15, 2005 Bear Sterns paid a $250 million fine to settle SEC allegations that the firm engaged in abusive mutual fund trading practices (Thomas Jr., 12/16/05). The $250 million fine was comprised of a $90 million penalty and the remainder was disgorgement set aside as restitution for affected shareholders (Weiss, 3/25/06). In addition to the monetary penalties, Bear Sterns committed to the hiring of independent consultants to review their internal controls in the clearing and mutual funds areas. The inclusion of stipulations such as hiring independent consultants was another common element in settlements, and is related to the practice of deferred prosecution, common to white-collar crime cases generally.

Deferred prosecution is similar to probation, in that the defendant agrees to a number of conditions over a set period of time. The difference is that instead of avoiding jail time, the offender avoids a trial altogether, so no one has to testify to their actions or introduce evidence of wrongdoing. If a defendant meets those conditions for the required period of time then any complaint, indictment, or investigation will be dismissed (Goldstein, 8/28/06). The advantage to this practice is that prosecutors save money and time by avoiding a trial, as well as eliminating the risk that a jury or judge will find the defendant not guilty. Prosecutors may also claim the ability to affect business practices, at least during the agreement's specified duration, better than simply getting a conviction or settlement. Despite these benefits, difficulties remain in preventing organizations from reverting to past behaviors after their probationary period. This is exemplified in the recent case of AIG's securities violations which are similar to their 2004 violations that received a deferred prosecution agreement with the Department of Justice (Department of Justice [DOJ], 11/4/04). There is also a question of whether deferred prosecution agreements make for easier cases if an offender recidivates during the period covered by their deferred prosecution agreement, as with probation/parole violations.

Records indicate that Bear Sterns made $20 million from their illegal trading and clearing room practices and Bear Sterns lawyers argued that their punishment should match their profits. The SEC countered that Bear Sterns provided a platform for abusive trading practices and facilitated actions which were essential to allowing the practices to continue (Goldstein, 11/13/03). Therefore, this represents an enhancement of the penalty application procedures due to what the SEC had termed "egregiousness of conduct". It also provides outsiders with a clearer understanding of regulatory agencies' priorities in punishing offenders.

Prudential

On August 28, 2006 the company, now known as Prudential Financial, paid a $600 million dollar fine for allowing their brokers to market time on behalf of hedge fund clients in several mutual funds. The $600 million consisted of $270 million paid to a SEC fund to compensate those victims of market timing, a $325 million dollar fine from the Department of Justice, and separate $5 million dollar fine from the Massachusetts Securities Division (NASD/FINRA, 8/26/06). Prudential's penalty tied for the second largest fine to come out of the mutual fund scandal-Alliance Capital received an equal fine in 2003. Prudential was also the first institution to admit to criminal wrongdoing as part of the mutual fund scandal (Thomas Jr., 8/29/06).

The settlement was part of a deferred prosecution agreement that will last five years and covers over $116 billion in trades made from January 2001 to July 2003, and netted $162 million in profits for at least 1,600 Prudential clients, including many hedge funds (NASD/FINRA, 8/26/06). The large amount of trades in this case demonstrates how a few brokers can cause a lot of damage within the industry. Investigations showed that the practices were also condoned by top executives, despite repeated complaints from mutual fund companies. In addition to the $600 million dollar penalty, Prudential is required to make periodic reports to the government regarding its compliance. Another unique term of this deferred prosecution arrangement was that Prudential Equity Group make a criminal admission of guilt, which opens the firm to greater liability from civil suits by shareholders or regulatory agencies.

In addition to the company fine, four brokers have been civilly sued by the SEC and face several potential punishments including: fines, returns of any monies made from the abusive trades, and bans from the securities industry (Thomas Jr., 8/29/06). Prudential fired the brokers during a period where it spun off its securities business into a joint venture with Wachovia and the mutual fund investigations were announced.

MFS Investment Management

Massachusetts Financial Services Investment Management (MFS), the eleventh largest American fund company at the time of the mutual fund scandal, actually invented the modern mutual fund in 1924. This is contrary to white-collar crime theory which posits that younger and/or smaller firms are more likely to engage in risky or unethical practices (Wheeler & Rothman, 1984). However, in February 2004 MFS reached a settlement with the SEC, New York Attorney General's office, and New Hampshire Bureau of Securities Regulation, to pay a $50 million fine, $175 million in disgorgement, and reduce their fees by $125 million over the next five years (SEC, 2/5/04). Like Putnam, MFS was also required to increase and enhance certain compliance and governance policies related to mutual fund oversight, including independence for their mutual fund board of trustees. Like Janus, MFS was required to pay an additional $1 million to the New Hampshire state regulators (Dugas, 2/5/04).

In addition to penalties against the company, MFS CEO John Ballen and President Kevin Parke were banned from working in the investment industry for three years, and were prohibited from associating with an investment adviser for nine and six months, respectively. They were also fined $250k and forced to disgorge $50k each (Dugas, 2/5/04). This was the first time during the scandal that a top mutual fund company executive had been fined.

The SEC found that MFS, including Ballen and Parke, were aware of approximately $2 billion in market timing assets within its firm in 2003. At the time, $2 billion represented 5% of all MFS assets. The SEC also discovered that MFS had deemed eleven of their mutual funds, "unrestricted funds." They permitted market timing and late trading in these funds, and even directed known market timers and late traders to these funds (SEC, 2/5/04). This case was also unusual in that there was no agreement regarding maintaining "sticky assets" at the firm while market timing with a smaller account. Instead, investors could market time with any or all of their accounts, within the unrestricted funds. These practices went above and beyond market timing and late trading at other mutual fund companies, in that this was an explicitly stated internal policy and not just a few actors working together within the company to subvert poorly enforced rules for profit.

Days after the settlement was released, MFS hired Robert Pozen, former vice chairman to Fidelity Investments and economic adviser to former Massachusetts Governor Mitt Romney, as their non-executive chairman (Dugas, 2/9/04). One month later, MFS announced that they were increasing transparency regarding fees. This is noteworthy because, by this time, the SEC had publicly stated that they were not interested in fee reductions as a part of mutual fund penalties and reforms. MFS's actions demonstrated that their public statement, in addition to trying to appease investors, was aimed at Spitzer and other state attorney generals, rather than federal regulators.

Security Trust

Spitzer alleged that Bank of America and the Security Trust Company made arrangements with Mr. Stern to allow his hedge fund to late trade in their mutual funds. This led the most severe punishment of an organization involved in the scandal, as Spitzer, the SEC, and the Department of Treasury's Office of the Comptroller of Currency (OCC) simultaneously brought actions against Security Trust (SEC, 11/25/03). The OCC regulators shut down the Security Trust Company in November 2003, representing the first and only organizational "death sentence" issued from the scandal. The OCC, the primary regulator of banks and trust companies, only participated in this one case, so it is difficult to compare their actions here to other cases. Nonetheless, Spitzer did charge former Security Trust executives with grand larceny, fraud, and falsification of records. Grand larceny, a class B felony, and six charges of grand larceny for each defendant represented 8 1/3 to 25 years of imprisonment (NYOAG, 11/25/03). Former Security Trust Senior Vice President Nicole McDermott pleaded guilty in December 2003 and was sentenced to four years in prison. Ex-CEO Grant Seeger and former President William Kenyon, initially pleaded not guilty to all 98 counts, but ultimately took a plea bargain in August 2005 in exchange for five years probation and $50,000 fines (Goldstein, 8/30/05). Severity of the penalties represented Security Trust's degree of involvement in illegal trading, as well as active participation from its management.

On March 21, 2004 a Federal District Court judge issued a $1 million penalty against Security Trust (SEC, 4/1/04). Records show that Canary Capital made an estimated $85 million from the late trading arrangement, while Security Trust made $5.8 million (Elkind, 4/19/04). While the disgorgement penalty does not equate to the estimated profits that Security Trust Company obtained from illegal trading, they did receive the ultimate penalty when their company was dissolved and their executives given probation or prison time.

Putnam

Putnam was the first mutual fund company to be charged with fraud as part of the mutual fund scandal. In October 2003 the SEC reached a settlement with Putnam Investments regarding their failure to detect or deter market timing of Putnam funds by their own fund managers. They were also charged with securities fraud for not revealing their managers' self-dealings (Morgensen, 11/16/03). Putnam's settlement included $110 million in combined fines and restitution to be paid to both the SEC and the state of Massachusetts, with $55 million going to each agency. Putnam also fired their former CEO Lawrence Lasser for personally benefiting from late trading in Putnam funds. Portfolio managers, Justin M. Scott and Omid Kamshad, were charged with excessive short term trading in Putnam mutual funds for personal profit. They settled the SEC's charges with a total fine of $1.5 million (SEC, 4/8/04).

While Putnam only received the fifteenth largest penalty, their crimes were among the worst, with illegal self-dealing by management. In addition, their case was settled relatively early in the scandal-seven months after the Canary Capital settlement. This indicates that either, according to the SEC's penalty formula, there were relatively few offenses committed and/or Putnam cooperated well with the regulatory agencies.   Also, the settlement being divided between two regulatory agencies made this case unusual. Outside of the $1 million additional penalties to states, no other cases indicated settlements being divided between federal and state regulators. It is possible that Massachusetts Attorney General, William Galvin, wanted to make a point in this case and increase the penalty at Putnam while also stealing some spotlight from the SEC. There was a public rift between Galvin and the SEC which will be examined further in subsequent chapters. This was also the perfect opportunity to try and upstage the SEC, as a former Putnam employee went to the SEC in April 2003 to complain about market timing only for the SEC to find no violations (Elkind, 4/19/04).

In addition to monetary penalties Putnam also agreed to make significant changes to their governance, compliance, and ethics programs. Putnam instituted short-term trading restrictions against their employees that range from 90 days to one year. Putnam will also require their Chief Compliance Officer to report all securities violations and breaches of fiduciary obligations to the independent board of directors. Putnam must maintain a code of ethics oversight committee to review any breaches and report them to the board of trustees. They must also create an internal compliance committee to review their compliance controls.   Putnam must also retain an independent compliance consultant to review their current controls regarding ethics and fiduciary duty, with a full third party review at least once every two years. They are also required to maintain independence of their board chairmen and three-quarters of the board's members-which they supposedly already had in place (SEC, 11/13/03).

Executives Stealing from the Company: "Control frauds"

The nature of market timing and late trading is similar in nature to that of collective embezzlement-identified by Pontell and Calavita (1994). They discovered this new crime-type while investigating the Savings and Loan during the early 1990's. Collective embezzlement occurs when the head of a company commits fraud for personal gain at the expense of their own company. This is what happened at mutual funds that allowed market timing and late trading, although the process was more complex because of the manner in which mutual funds operate. Mutual funds are investment vehicles and not financial institutions and thus managers needed to collaborate with wealthy investors in order to conduct their fraud (except in those cases where the mutual fund managers were the ones doing the illegal trading).

Two prominent cases of this recent version of collective embezzlement include Pilgrim & Baxter (PBHG) and Richard Strong's Strong Funds. The founders of these two firms allowed market timing and late trading in their funds. They were also playing both sides of the illegal trades, benefiting from the "sticky assets" and from the illegal trading profits. Although they took slightly different approaches to committing fraud, proceeds were looted because their owners conducted illegal trades at the expense of their clients.

Pilgrim Baxter & Associates

Pilgrim Baxter & Associates (PBHG) was founded in 1982 and, as of September 30, 2003, held $7.4 billion in assets under management. As mentioned above, the PBHG mutual fund family also saw their founders involved in illegal trading within their own fund. Gary Pilgrim managed the company's PBHG Growth Fund, which allowed the hedge fund Appalachian Trail to engage in market timing within the Growth Fund. Both Pilgrim and his wife also had a stake in Appalachian Trail, which traded the PBHG Growth fund an estimated 120 times from March 2000 through November 2001. This easily exceeded the eight in-and-out trades that PBHG would allows for its investors over the two-year period (Sloan, 12/8/03). During this period of time, the Growth fund declined 65% in value, yet Pilgrim made an estimated $3.9 million (a 49% profit) from his investment in the market timing hedge fund. At least some of this profit was also earned because Pilgrim used his inside knowledge of the mutual fund's holdings to short sell the mutual fund, similar to the illegal strategy used by Eddie Stern and Canary Capital (Newsweek, 12/08/03). Appalachian Trail made an estimated $13 million from its trading in the Growth fund, much of it while the mutual fund was actually decreasing in value. It is also believed that, at the height of market timing in the Growth Fund, 11% of the funds' total assets were being used to engage in market timing (Dugas, 11/20/03). Pilgrim's stake in Appalachian Trail represented a clear violation of his fiduciary responsibility. He was legally required to put his shareholder's interests first, but he broke these legal obligations by giving priority to his personal financial stake in the hedge fund that was short selling his mutual fund.

In November 2004 the co-founders of Pilgrim Baxter & Associates (PBHG) were each ordered to pay $20 million in civil penalties and $60 million in restitution. Both then resigned as executives from their mutual fund company. This penalty was coupled with a $50 million dollar civil penalty and $40 million in disgorgement against the organization paid in June 2004 to settle with regulators (CNN, 11/17/04). This money was distributed to PBHG's investors harmed by market timing. In addition to the fines, Baxter and Pilgrim are permanently banned from future employment in the securities industry.

This was one of the earlier settlements in the lifespan of the scandal, in part because it was connected to Canary Capital, and therefore, it was discovered early. The SEC took note of the egregiousness of these offenses during the press release announcing the settlement. Stephen Cutler, Director of the SEC's Division of Enforcement, said, "The amounts being paid in this settlement are virtually unprecedented for individuals in civil cases. Along with the permanent bars, the monetary sanctions we have obtained here reflect the severity of the misconduct and the fundamental breach of duty at issue in this case (SEC, 11/17/04)." Pilgrim and Baxter's lifetime bans, as well as the large individual and organizational fines demonstrate how regulatory organizations punished offenses where upper management was involved in self-dealing.

Strong

Spitzer subpoenaed the company and discovered that, in addition to the involvement with Canary Capital, the founder and Chief Executive, Richard Strong, had been market timing with his personal account for the previous five years. Strong had been averaging about two dozen trades a year, most of which were in and out trades spanning a couple of days each. His strategy was to purchase mid- and small-cap funds when the market was in an upswing, betting that it would take a couple of days for those stocks' value to reflect the upward movement of the market. The problem was that Strong funds have a 1% penalty for funds that were held less than one year and they blacklist traders that trade out within thirty days of purchasing their mutual fund. This penalty was not applied to Canary Capital Partners or Richard Strong, himself. No official indication was given that late trading had occurred at Strong funds, but regulators did determine that Richard Strong earned an estimated $600,000 to $1.8 million in profits through market timing his funds (Smith, 10/30/03).

Richard Strong founded Strong Financial Corporation in 1974 and, at its peak; he managed $42 billion in assets, including $1 billion in college savings plans-which had been entrusted by the state of Wisconsin. Strong was listed also on the Forbes 400 with a net worth of $800 million (Smith, 10/30/03). When the investigation became public Strong retired from the company's board of directors, but he remained as the company's chief executive officer-a position he resigned in December 2003. Spitzer discovered that Strong had bypassed the company's internal controls by assigning the company's internal regulators to watch over Strong's larger funds while he market timed the smaller funds. Further investigations by the SEC and Department of Labor uncovered hundreds of illegal trades that Strong had approved for various pension plans (Smith, 10/30/2003).

In addition to market timing discoveries, Strong Capital's brochure for their institutional investors discloses that the company also participates in several other legal, but ethically questionable practices. These practices include: receiving payments and discounts from brokers in exchange for processing trades, accepting stock prices above the market value in exchange for research and other benefits, and allocating "hot" IPOs to hedge fund clients-who pay higher fees-rather than to mutual fund clients (Atlas, 5/21/04).

Despite Strong's public statement of contrition, his associates recalled several statements which showed him as willing to engage in risky or illegal business behavior. They remember him often using sayings like, "This is a business not a church" and "If I can get away with it, why not?" (Smith, 10/30/03). There were other signs that Strong Capital had problems. Ron Ognar, one of Strong's most trusted money managers and a Strong employee for the previous ten years, left suddenly and without explanation. It is now known that Ognar managed four of the five funds identified by Spitzer as having been market timed (Smith, 10/30/03).

The Supreme Court Rules

In June 2011, in the case of *Janus Capital Group v. First Derivative Traders*, the Supreme Court ruled on an issue related to the civil suits against the mutual fund companies whose prospectuses prohibited market timing, but allowed the practice for certain customers. The issue at hand was who could be considered liable for making the false statements, and therefore, would be financially liable to the injured parties. In a 5-4 decision the court ruled that only the entity that made the actual statement would be liable, even if they were part of a larger group. In this case, Janus Capital Group and Janus Capital Management are the actual entities involved and hold all the assets, even their business trust is technically responsible for writing the prospectus. Despite their inextricable connection and the common sense notion that the whole company is responsible for the legal documents that it publishes, Justice Thomas wrote for the majority that only the business trust may be held liable for the false statements in the prospectus (NY Times Editorial, June 14, 2011). So despite agreeing to pay out over $100 million in organizational fines and disgorgement and agreeing to $125 million in fee reductions, the Supreme Court has deemed that Janus is not liable for the market timing because an entity that Janus created to hold the mutual funds 'made' the statements in the prospectus. The Supreme Court has essentially decided that Janus is not civilly liable to those investors and investment companies they harmed by allowing market timing.

This case began in the District Court where the judge dismissed the complaint from First Derivative, ruling that they had failed to make a claim against Janus. The Fourth Circuit Court of Appeals reversed the original decision, finding that because Janus Capital Management and

Capital Group had participated in the writing and dissemination of the prospectuses they were liable for making the statements (McGrath, 6/13/2011). The Court's ruling was based upon the corporate structure of the organization and that only the business trust had the statutory obligation to file a prospectus, despite the fact that Janus Capital Group and Capital Management actually contributed to the prospectus. This finding will ultimately limit a citizen's ability to recover financial damages from similar future cases and may impair regulators' ability to compel organizations into paying compensation, if financial firms feel that they can exploit the Court's ruling to make them not liable for actions within their organization.

CHAPTER 3

Spitzer and the New York Attorney General's Office

On September 3, 2003, Spitzer went public with his investigation of market timing and late trading in the mutual fund industry. That announcement represented the first notice by a regulatory agency that there was an ongoing investigation into fund industry practices. The SEC, FINRA, federal prosecutors, and state regulators soon joined with Spitzer. Between all regulatory agencies and actors, hundreds of defendants have been charged or have reached settlements. As Spitzer said, "[Eddie Stern has] given us 20 or 30 names of mutual funds and 20 or 30 names of hedge funds (Elkind, 4/19/04)." This supposes that at least 40 to 60 organizations were involved in illegal or unethical practices with Canary Capital alone. The result of this scandal would expose wrongdoing in more than one hundred investment companies. It was the largest scandal ever to afflict the mutual fund industry, and the combined penalties from settlements represented almost $5.4 billion.

Eliot Spitzer took the market timing and late trading scandal into national prominence. He had already made a name for himself as a crusader against white-collar, specifically Wall Street offenders. He had already stared down big banks, Merrill Lynch and Citigroup, and reaching settlements regarding conflicts of interest in their investment and research divisions. However, taking on the mutual fund industry would be a real test for the New York Attorney General, as this was considered a venerable, scandal-free industry. Luckily, circumstances were made easier for Spitzer due to revelations of several other major white-collar scandals in the two to three years preceding the market timing and late trading scandal. These predecessors and their continual, front page exposure likely conditioned the public into accepting that financial organizations were often involved in scandals.

Despite indications of forty to sixty offenders, which the former Canary Capital head provided   to the New York Attorney General, Spitzer's office only reached settlements with a total of twenty-two organizations. In addition, eight investigations provided eleven criminal cases, which resulted in ten guilty pleas and one trial. There were also at least two individuals who faced charges related to market timing and late trading who eventually had their charges dropped. It is likely that many more were investigated, although exact numbers are unknown.

Spitzer's Work in White-Collar Crime

Eliot Spitzer's Political Career Arc

Before Eliot Spitzer publicized the late trading and market timing scandal, he was already well known for his efforts investigating and prosecuting white-collar offenders. He became New York's Attorney General in January 1999. Within the first year, he sued seventeen Midwestern and Mid-Atlantic coal-fired power plants for violating the federal Clean Air Act. He filed a similar suit in July 2000, against Virginia Power, as their modifications to a Mount Storm plant were in violation of the same Clean Air Act (Perez-Pena, 11/16/00). In April 2002 he sued Merrill Lynch for conflicts of interest between their investment analysts and brokers, and a settlement followed in May. By September he filed a similar suit against Citigroup, publicizing conflicts of interest existing within many financial companies' research and investment banking divisions. His office was able to show how companies used their investment recommendations as a weapon to earn business, bolster investments made by other divisions within the organization, or harm other organizations that did not give business to the investment firm. He discovered emails that demonstrated clear acts of collusion to deceive investors, and his office calculated that analysts were issuing "sell" recommendations in less than .4% of the eight thousand recommendations that they made. These cases resulted in a large global plea between Spitzer's office and the major firms of Wall Street, in which they all paid a percentage of the $1.4 billion penalty and agreed to structural reforms designed to address the conflicts of interest (SEC, 12/20/02).

The research analyst cases represented the beginning of Spitzer's conflicts with the SEC. Spitzer's office handled the case without consulting the SEC, and left them scrambling to catch up with the Attorney General's office findings, much like they did during the mutual fund scandal. In fact, as rumors of a pending case being filed against Merrill caused the company to contact the SEC to reason with Spitzer (Gasparino, 2005, p. 249). Spitzer's solo discovery and response to these cases damaged the reputation of the SEC, although perhaps rightly so if it was the case that the regulatory agency was acting as mediator between Wall Street offenders and prosecutors. The feud between the SEC and Spitzer continued as each group sought to take the lead and outdo each other on reforming Wall Street research, while trying to claim the best interests of the small investor. The fight escalated when Morgan Stanley executive Phil Purcell began advocating for Congress to introduce legislation that barred state officials from regulating Wall Street (Gasparino, 2005, p. 249). When SEC chairperson at the time, Harvey Pitt, did not argue strongly against the measure, Spitzer spoke out about the lack of leadership at the SEC and the missed cases which the New York Attorney General had discovered. Spitzer continued to preempt SEC cases with his own. Whether this was a case of political opportunism as SEC directors claimed, or simply that Spitzer was more prepared and aggressive than his regulatory counterparts is unclear. However, it is clear that this was upsetting the relationship between the two groups (Gasparino, 2005, pp. 279-280).

Spitzer then followed a lead uncovered in the Citigroup case and sued former head of WorldCom, Bernie Ebbers, and four other executives for their illegal arrangements. The New York Attorney General's office discovered that the CEO's were offering future business to the investment banks in exchange for popular initial public offerings of stock (Gasparino, 2005). Soon after these cases concluded, Spitzer reached a settlement with Canary Capital partners and began his investigations into the mutual fund scandal. He also began an investigation into the accounting practices at AIG, which resulted in the company's board removing CEO Hank Greenberg. Spitzer later challenged NYSE Chairperson Richard Grasso over his compensation which numbered in the tens of millions, despite the NYSE being classified as a non-profit. This investigation resulted in Grasso stepping down from the NYSE and returning some of his salary (Gasparino, 2005). It is both a testimony to the power of Wall Street and the history of white-collar prosecutions that Eliot Spitzer could build a reputation as a champion against corporate crime and draw such ire from the business community in a mere five years.

However, Spitzer's star fell as quickly as it rose. As Governor of New York and being mentioned as a possible Presidential candidate, he soon faced his own scandal. In March 2008, just fifteen months after being elected, he was identified as a client in a prostitution ring. Almost immediately, he resigned his position as Governor and stepped away from the political spotlight. He has since re-emerged as a lecturer at City College of New York and then as co-host of a show on CNN, but as he said in a recent interview, "Mistakes I made in my private life now prevent me from participating in [policy reform] as I have in the past (Spitzer, 11/16/08)." However, that time he spent combating white-collar crime and reforming policy has had an impact, as evidenced by rule changes and structural reforms on Wall Street, as well as monies refunded to defrauded investors.

Spitzer as Moral Entrepreneur

The term "moral entrepreneur" was coined by Howard S. Becker (1963) who defined such persons as those who seek to influence a group to adopt or maintain a norm. The moral entrepreneur may press for the creation or enforcement of a norm for any number of reasons, altruistic or selfish. Although scholars have often applied the moral entrepreneur label in medicine (Conrad & Schneider, 1992; Freidson, 1988), there are several historical examples of moral entrepreneurs in large social movements: prohibitionists who led the movement to make the United States a dry country, abolitionists who sought to ban slavery, or the temperance movement that led several humanitarian movements during the 1800's (Becker, 1963, p. 149; Gusfield, 1955, p. 223; McCarthy, 1959, pp. 395-396). While the humanitarian label does not apply to all moral entrepreneurs, they generally believe their actions will ultimately improve some aspects of life.

Only those in the upper social strata of society are successful in their moral crusades (Becker, 1963, p. 149). There is political competition in which these moral crusaders originate movements aimed at generating reform, based on what they think is moral and therefore necessarily define those who stand for something different as deviant. Moral crusaders must have power, public support, generate public awareness of the issue, and be able to propose a clear and acceptable solution to the problem (Becker, 1963). The qualifications for a moral crusader restrict those that may enter into this classification of individuals.

Over the course of Eliot Spitzer's tenure as New York State Attorney General, he was responsible for bringing a multitude of prominent white-collar crime cases and settlements. He also repeatedly talked about wresting power from corporations:

> We went after fewer individuals because it was a structural issue. We pursued no individual analysts, because they were cogs in the system and the system had failed and the regulators had failed. I would say we won in that we highlighted, sequentially, the fundamental problems of the investment banks, insurance companies, mutual funds, and on and on. During the eight years I was there we tried to shine a light on a regulatory and ideological framework that was wrong (BBC, 11/14/09).

Spitzer's efforts in this area demonstrated his commitment to controlling rampant free-market extravagance and abuse by trying to re-establish a sense of legal and regulatory control through proactive, white-collar investigations and prosecutions.

This approach towards white-collar offenses made Spitzer a moral entrepreneur. Becker defines a moral entrepreneur as a "crusading reformer" who does not feel that existing rules fulfill their ability to control some aspect of society that they feel is "evil" (Becker, 1963). "The moral crusader, however, is more concerned with ends rather than with means (Becker, 1963, p. 150)." In fact, in a recent BBC interview Spitzer indirectly referred to himself as a 'moral crusader'.

> This is a morality tale, and I have been on the right side of it on many cases, and the wrong side of it in others. It has been very difficult to watch and not participate given its cataclysmic effect. I was viewed as a heretic; as someone who did not understand markets. I said, 'No'. It is you who do not understand markets.'...If more people had acted as I did, we may not have had the cataclysm that we did. Time and again we stood up, but, I thought, with a thoughtfulness designed to create the appropriate remedy. I think the idea of self-regulation is one of those ideas we should discard along with

blood-letting as a form of medicine. It had its ideological moment. People believed in it, but hopefully we have moved on. It did not work (BBC, 11/14/09).

The idea that he recognized his own place within the greater framework of law and morality may have added to his motivation to continue pushing for punishment and reform.

Spitzer's internally driven approach to regulating business is consistent with Becker's description of moral entrepreneurs, "[The moral entrepreneur] believes that if they do what is right it will be good for them (Becker, 1963, p. 148)." The moral entrepreneur's motive may be to elevate the social status of those members of society below them. During his relatively short tenure as New York Attorney General, Spitzer certainly did not pander to the power elite. While investigating the conflicts between investment banking and research departments on Wall Street a lawyer from Merrill Lynch told him verbatim, 'Eliot, be careful. We have powerful friends.' (BBC, 11/14/09).

Becker makes a distinction between, what he calls "rule creators" and "rule enforcers". The rule creator is a crusader who is focused on the content of rules. They are not satisfied with the current state of rules, and hope to improve them to remedy some offense. The rule enforcer may not be interested in the content of the rule, as much as the fact that the rule provides the enforcer with a job. As Becker states, "[The rule enforcer's] attitude toward his work, in short, is professional. He lacks the naive moral fervor characteristic of the rule creator (Becker, 1963, p. 159)." While Spitzer did crusade against white-collar offenders, utilizing obscure laws and statutes to not only bring cases against these individuals and organizations, but also to justify that he had the jurisdictional authority to bring these cases in the first place. While this was productive in that he brought cases that held up to legal scrutiny, it may represent a challenge to Becker's typology of rule creators. Spitzer was not actually dissatisfied as much with the current state of rules as he was dissatisfied with the current state of society and regulation of business practices. As he put it, "I do not want to paint myself as some hero riding his stead into the teeth of the cavalry. I was just doing my job. (BBC, 11/14/09)". He drew upon existing laws and authorities granted to him as a state attorney general to combat injustices on Wall Street. His use of the Mann Act, an obscure 1920's securities law, was an example of how he worked within the system to expand how laws were used, rather than creating new laws.

The problem with this classification is that Spitzer is not a fit for the traditional rule enforcer label, even though it is likely closer in scope to his job description. Rule enforcers, according to Becker, "have two interests which condition his enforcement activity: first, he must justify the existence of his position and second, he must win the respect of those he deals with (Becker, 1963, p. 156)." As attorney general of New York, he was tasked with enforcing the rules of New York State. Spitzer's office prosecuted common criminals, in addition to any proactive work he accomplished against organizational offenders. It was only when he extended the normal range of prosecutorial responsibility and range of cases did people begin to pay attention to the work he was doing.

This situation represents an interesting paradox, as technically, Spitzer's job title may have categorized him as a rule enforcer. However, as state attorney general he also maintained a high level of authority and autonomy in setting his prosecutorial agenda and determining which issues received attention. He also had the ability to take a proactive or reactive stance in addressing different issues and types of crime. All the while, he was a political figure in an elected position, and responsible to his constituents, although he did not have the ability of a legislator or Governor to create or advocate for new laws. Also, he seemed to favor the idea that current regulatory organizations work better, rather than having lawmakers create new agencies and regulations. As stated in a recent column, "While new regulation may have meaningful results, it also encourages us to ignore more potent, and necessary, approaches to remedying the markets' structural problems" (Spitzer, 3/16/10). All of this seems to indicate that Spitzer may have fit the rare typology of a crusading rule enforcer, which Becker briefly alludes to in his work, "Although some policemen undoubtedly have a kind of crusading interest in stamping out evil, it is probably much more typical for the policeman to have a certain detached and objective view of his job" (Becker, 1963, p. 156).

Adding to the confusion over Spitzer's true classification is the effect of his work as attorney general of New York. According to Becker, the success of a crusade may transition moral entrepreneurs into the role of a professional rule creator (Becker, 1963). As discussed above, Spitzer gained immense popularity while prosecuting Wall Street and this popularity led him to an easy win in the race for Governor of New York, or professional rule creator at the state level.

The effect of moral entrepreneurship, according to Becker, is the formation of a new class of outsiders whose behavior now violates these newly minted regulations and therefore is subject to the label of "deviant." In *Outsiders: Studies in the Sociology of Deviance* (1963), Becker elaborates on the concept of moral entrepreneurs through a case study of US marijuana laws. He identifies the Federal Bureau of Narcotics as a rule creator that mobilized its considerable resources to initiate a powerful moral crusade against marijuana use (*Blackwell Encyclopedia of Sociology*). Becker believes that the final outcome of a moral crusade is the creation of a new set of rules and a police force (Becker, 1963). This is an interesting effect, as it implies that the moral crusade against white-collar crime took place in the era of the Great Depression, and likely included Sutherland and others, as they turned it into a national issue and became an advocate of new rules and regulations for corporations and executives. Consequently, those like Spitzer, who came after, may be better classified as "rule enforcers". As rules against market timing and late trading were already in place, but were simply not being enforced.

The other option is that Spitzer and others like him are not neatly categorized as either a rule creators or rule enforcers. It is also possible that more than one group of rule creating moral entrepreneurs need to exist for an issue to stay salient. As those that oppose the original rule creator may work against that particular wave of moral entrepreneurship and attempt to reverse the original entrepreneur's achievements. This process would be more consistent with what way know about law creation, in that it is not a linear path for creation and enforcement, but rather a constant process of forward and backward movement (Chambliss, 1993)

Without Spitzer There Would Have Been No Scandal

Over the course of the market timing and late trading scandal, Eliot Spitzer and his New York Attorney General's office prosecuted ten mutual fund companies, four of the five hedge funds who reached settlements and other investment companies, and imposed a total of over $4 billion in penalties, including fines, disgorgements, and fee reductions. In addition, forty-five fiduciaries were banned from the securities industry, ten individuals pleaded guilty, one individual was acquitted, and one company was dissolved-although the dissolution was officially ordered by the Office of the Comptroller of the Currency.

Spitzer was involved in twenty-two market timing and late trading cases, which resulted in approximately $4.45 billion in penalties, which represents only 35% of the total cases, but just over 80% of the total penalties levied from the scandal. However, that number could really be 100%, as these abuses likely would have gone undiscovered without Eliot Spitzer.

Spitzer's Weapon

The Martin Act – a New York State securities law created in 1921 and commonly used to prosecute bogus stock sales and boiler room establishments – became one of Spitzer's primary weapons in pursuing white-collar offenders (McTamaney, 2003). The Martin Act is a state law that, unlike federal laws, does not require prosecutors to allege intent before filing charges. Instead, prosecutors need only show an appearance of criminal intentions, "such as an undisclosed conflict of interest (Gasparino, 2005, p. 215)." This is exactly what Spitzer had with the market timing and late trading scandal, which allowed him to file charges against the various organizations, without indicating whether the case is civil or criminal in nature, and put pressure on them to settle. An especially powerful weapon, because no major securities company has ever survived a criminal prosecution.

Spitzer's Investigation of the Fund Industry

Whistleblower, Noreen Harrington, admitted that she did not feel confident approaching the SEC or other regulatory body to talk about what she had learned from Canary Capital (Elkind, 4/19/04). She feared that these other organizations would not act upon her information and investors would continue to suffer. Spitzer, however, already had a reputation as a champion of white-collar prosecutions. By the summer of 2003 he had already reached settlements with corporate polluters and self-dealing investment banks. In addition to making himself available for whistleblowers to confess their organizational sins, Spitzer was a pro-active prosecutor. Early in his tenure as Attorney General for New York State, Spitzer sat down with David Brown, head of the state's investor protection bureau, and asked him which would be the next area to investigate. Brown recalled an academic paper he had seen about arbitrage opportunities and trading irregularities in mutual funds (Atlas, 12/27/03). So the scandal was actually discovered by whistleblowers, the media, and academics, who understood what was happening in the mutual fund industry. However, as Howard Becker stated, "[E]nforcement occurs when those who want the rule enforced publicly bring the infraction to the attention of others (Becker, 1963, p. 122)." Of course, these people have to be in position to enforce the rule, as the original whistleblower that approached the SEC wanted the rule enforced, but the SEC did not bring the infraction to the attention of others. Without a person like Spitzer in that place at that time, it is doubtful that the SEC, FINRA, or any other financial regulator would have ever discovered the scandal. The federal regulatory bodies had not discovered any malfeasance up to that point, despite other whistleblowers having approached them with information.

The Prudential case provides insight into how likely watchdogs and informers had done in exposing the late trading and market timing scandal. There are records of thousands of complaints from fund companies to brokerage firms, as fund company compliance officers warned brokerages about illegal trading or notified them that they had been blocked from further trading in that fund. As explained by the Massachusetts Secretary of State, and the state's top securities regulator, William F Galvin,

> There were many mutual fund companies whose timing police officers, backed up by senior compliance executives, successfully rebuffed the market timers who approached them, regulators said...But not even healthy compliance programs encouraged anyone to take 'the logical next step, which was to blow the whistle. It looks to me like a conspiracy of silence in the fund industry," Mr. Galvin said in an interview, "If everyone knew what was happening – and documented it, as in the case of these compliance officers who complained to Prudential – why didn't anyone take steps to stop it? (Henriques, 12/11/03)."

Instead, Mr. Galvin's investigators received their first tip about Prudential's Boston brokers from a disgruntled employee. By then the larger scandal had been exposed by Spitzer. However, this case reveals two elements that highlight Eliot Spitzer's importance for investigating and prosecuting the mutual fund scandal. First, that an employee whistleblower had been rebuffed by the federal regulators suggests that it was unlikely that the agency would revisit their decision not to prosecute these cases. Second, the discovery of more than 25,000 emails between sixty-six different mutual fund companies and Prudential over a twelve month period asking that Prudential stop these abusive practices indicates that mutual fund compliance departments were not going to involve regulators in these acts (Goldstein, 8/2/05). The lack of action by federal regulators as well as the mutual fund companies victimized by these actions left this scandal to be uncovered by a more aggressive and non-conventional type of enforcement agent.

Spitzer made mutual fund cases a priority and his office conducted investigations without involving any other outside agencies. On September 3, 2003 when Spitzer announced the settlement with Canary Capital Partners and continuing investigations into other mutual fund cases the SEC and NASD learned of the news the same way the average investor did, through the media (Sender & Zuckerman, 2003). It was only after hearing this news and calling Spitzer did the SEC and NASD/FINRA become involved in investigating and prosecuting mutual fund abuses. SEC Chairperson William Donaldson noted that, "You have to remember, during the bull market there were other things going on in the mutual funds that we were working on, and we've had a number of things that we've been working on well before Eliot Spitzer came along. But in terms of this specific issue of late trading and market timing, you know, we were not there" (PBS, 11/26/03). From that point both regulatory agencies were active participants in cases from that point forward. Either the SEC or NASD/FINRA participated in 58 of 62 settlements, not including Canary Capital Partners.

Despite the participation of federal regulatory agencies in almost every case, Eliot Spitzer was responsible for the prosecutions. This was a result of the lone wolf nature of Spitzer's campaign against white-collar crime which he had established during his short career as the New York Attorney General.   For example, there were predetermined SEC guidelines stemming from The Securities Enforcement Remedies and Penny Stock Reform Act of 1990 which indicated the quantity and quality of punishment applicable to mutual fund and investment companies in the market timing and late trading scandal. However, both the regulatory agencies and Spitzer's office also negotiated penalties that regularly included revocation of individual investment licenses as well as multi-year or even lifetime banishment from working in the securities industry. The hallmark and most controversial element of Spitzer's cases were fee reductions which his office included in approximately two-thirds of their settlements. A typical Spitzer negotiated settlement would include a fine, disgorgement of profits earned from market timing and/or late trading, and a five-year reduction of company fees.   Fourteen cases involved fee reductions, with a range of $5 million to $350 million, and an average of over $75 million.   This type of punishment, while not directly related to the offense, was an immediate benefit to the customer which may have been originally harmed by the company.   It also suborned the company to the customer, which was a common theme in Spitzer's settlements.   Incorporating these elements into his settlements demonstrated Spitzer's intention to help investors and control the market rather than simply punish white-collar criminals or uncover fraud, although also he accomplished those objectives.

Overview of Spitzer Cases

Outside of the Canary Capital case, all of Spitzer's mutual fund prosecutions were done in collaboration with the SEC and NASD, among other agencies.   Despite the joint settlements, an animosity between Spitzer and the regulatory agencies remained.   This appeared to be a continuation of enmity that began when Spitzer embarrassed the SEC by grabbing headlines with the analyst cases only the year before. As discussed above, in the analyst cases, not only did Spitzer tread onto SEC jurisdiction, but he was able to extract larger and more expansive settlements than the SEC ever had.   This was a trend that continued into the market timing and late trading scandal.

One feature of Spitzer's approach to mutual fund abuses is that he seemed to only pursue high profile cases which involved prominent companies, resulted in large fines, or were criminal cases with possible jail time attached.   Having the benefit of hindsight with regard to Eliot Spitzer's political run that followed soon after the mutual fund scandal, it is reasonable to infer that Spitzer's motivations in case selection may have been politically motivated.   Of course, his political ambitions also benefited the general public through exposure and prosecution of mutual fund abuses.

The cases that Spitzer brought and settled were primarily born of a spider's web emanating from Canary Capital.   As mentioned in the opening of this chapter, Canary and Eddie Stern provided Spitzer with information on dozens of market timing and late trading co-conspirators.   For example, while Canary traded in PBHG funds, they also used Bank of America's trading platform to conduct the trades, and Security Trust Company to clear the trades.   All three of these companies had direct connections to Canary in these illegal operations and all three were among the most heavily penalized organizations from this scandal. Others directly connected to Canary include, but are not limited to: Strong Mutual Funds, Federated Shareholders, Banc One Investments, PIMCO entities, and Kaplan & Company, representing almost a third of all Spitzer late trading and/or market timing cases. This list does not include those tangentially related to Canary, including those that may have shared illegal trading methodologies or illegal trading in the same entities and were discovered after investigations into another organization.

Criminal Cases

Spitzer was the driving force between criminal prosecutions of mutual fund abuses. Of these eleven criminal cases, ten resulted in convictions, all from plea bargains. The one non-conviction, the Sihpol case, which resulted in a hung jury and the case was never re-tried, was as a black mark on Spitzer's record. Some media analysts and industry professionals even called that case the end of Spitzer's crusade against the mutual fund industry. Despite these claims, Spitzer's office obtained three more guilty pleas and several settlements after the Sihpol setback. Much of his continued success settling cases was due to collaborative efforts during the entire scandal, with the SEC, NASD/FINRA, and other state attorney generals all involved in multiple settlements of mutual fund cases. Public announcements of cases were consistently described as "joint settlements" or "brought in conjunction with," and the SEC announcements all thanked the efforts of Spitzer's office, and/or whichever state-level regulator or self-regulatory body aided in developing and prosecuting the case.

Despite this multi-agency approach, or, as Braithwaite (1995) termed it, a legal-pluralist model of regulation, all criminal cases involved the New York State Attorney General's office. However, it is difficult to categorize this as proof Spitzer was acting outside of the legal-pluralist approach, as the SEC and those involved SROs are only legally permitted to bring civil cases or administrative cases against organizations or individuals. This would have prevented them from joining with Spitzer in his criminal cases. However, the SEC is allowed to make criminal referrals to the Department of Justice for specific cases, and there is a possibility that there could be some collaboration between state and federal prosecutors in terms of information sharing

(E.G. Osterman, personal communication, 7/23/08). Nonetheless, the SEC is not mentioned as contributing or assisting in any stories or press releases regarding Spitzer's criminal cases regarding market timing and late trading.

Criminal Convictions

The ten criminal convictions were all plea agreements on various charges. They included two cases of tampering or destroying evidence related to the mutual fund investigation. In both of these cases the guilty individuals were high ranking officials within the company. The eight remaining cases all involved charges from New York's Martin Act/General Business Law-Eliot Spitzer's powerful state law which allowed him flexibility in charging and prosecuting white-collar crime. The one exception was an individual from the Security Trust Company case who was also pleaded to Second Degree Larceny in addition to the Martin Act charges. The guilty parties included employees ranging from brokers to senior officials and executives, including a CEO, President, and other executives.

One Acquittal

It would have been a significant case for Spitzer's record and public image, given the amount of media attention the case had received. Spitzer brought thirty-three counts against Sihpol, which carried a possible maximum of thirty years in prison. A jury who returned this sentence would have demonstrated either understanding of complex offenses perpetrated between high-level business persons, or general outrage at corruption in the financial system. Either way, this could have represented at least a temporary sea change in the nature of white-collar crime prosecutions, and may have cleared the way for future white-collar cases. However, the State Supreme Court of Manhattan dismissed twenty-nine of the original thirty-three charges, and the jury hung on the remaining four charges. Eliot Spitzer, who had already begun his campaign for Govenor of New York, never re-filed charges against Sihpol (Atlas & Abelson, 6/10/05).

Critics and political or ideological opponents to Spitzer and his policies seized on the acquittal to suggest that Spitzer and his mission were beginning to fail. "I think this is a major blow to Eliot Spitzer and his campaign against Wall Street, "said Robert G. Heim, a former lawyer with the SEC, who is now a partner at Meyers & Heim.

Ironically, similar claims were made a year earlier after Spitzer had convened a grand jury to consider criminal charges against Strong, but the case was not pursued. Roy Weitz who runs the website FundAlarm.com states, "Mr. Spitzer had been holding up Strong as a poster child for going to jail. There's some suggestion that the steam is running out of this investigation," with regulators eager to settle and move to other matters (Atlas, 5/21/04).

Others viewed the Sihpol case as a minor or insignificant setback in the larger picture of Spitzer's accomplishments. Roland G. Riopelle, a former federal prosecutor who practices law at Sercarz & Riopelle, said Mr. Spitzer was responsible for a sweeping overhaul of the mutual fund industry. "He's accomplished a hell of a lot long before this case went to the jury," he said. Darren Dopp, a spokesman for Spitzer said, "We implemented sweeping reforms. Late trading and market timing are outlawed practices. We lost this case, but efforts to bring accountability in the mutual fund industry continue. Our record over the last two years speaks for itself." Perhaps most telling were the statements from Paul Schectman, a lawyer for Theodore Sihpol, who said, "This should not be read as a jury saying that what Eliot Spitzer has done is for naught. There is no doubt that he has spoken on important conflicts of interest and he has been an aggressive and successful attorney general. But when you bring a criminal indictment, you have to prove it, and on this one, he didn't" (Atlas & Abelson, 6/10/05). Despite these claims, Spitzer and company continued mutual fund investigations, convicting three more individuals and reaching settlements in another seven cases.

Strong Capital

For his part in the mutual fund scandal, Richard Strong was fined $60 million dollars, which was the highest fine for an individual, as part of the scandal. In addition, Strong Capital paid an $80 million dollar fine and cut management fees by 6% for the next five years. Spitzer has commented on speculation about his decision not to pursue criminal action against Strong, "the criminal cases we've made all relate to late trading," he said, which refers to trades made after the market has closed but which still receive the previous day's price. Such trading is clearly illegal, Spitzer said, but the legality of market timing is more ambiguous (Atlas & Abelson, 6/10/05). These difficulties in prosecutorial decision-making may reflect a lack of comprehensive securities law as well as complications in handling white-collar and financial crime cases, a sentiment which has been often discussed in white-collar crime research. The literature supports the view that the complexity of evidence and the capacity of wealthy defendants to mobilize legal talent makes prosecuting white-collar offenders more difficult (Levi, 1981).

In addition to the large financial penalties, and in spite of not pressing criminal action, Spitzer did require that Strong issue a statement of contrition, rather than the standard "refusal to admit or deny charges" common in other cases. This was an unusual step in the plea agreement, and offered the only case where an individual involved in the scandal was forced to admit wrongdoing. Forcing this admission may open Richard Strong to civil lawsuits by shareholders of Strong mutual funds. It is also possible that Spitzer made this distinction with Strong given that Strong was the CEO of the mutual fund company, while personally profiting from these practices. Spitzer confirms this by saying, "The magnitude of his breach of duty is greater than what we have seen in other cases (Atlas, 5/21/04)." However, a similar situation appears to have been present at PBHG, where Gary Pilgrim and his wife were 50% owners of a hedge fund called Appalachian Trail, which was allowed to market time in one the PBHG mutual funds. It was also possible that the statement of contrition was an element desired by Spitzer, as he pressed for a similar concession from individuals involved in the stock analyst cases (Gasparino, 2005).

Canadian Imperial Bank of Commerce

In November 2005, Spitzer dropped the charges against CIBC trader Paul A. Flynn. This occurred approximately one month after the remaining four charges had been dropped against Theodore Sihpol III. Spitzer's office issued an order to the New York State Supreme Court arguing that recent guilty pleas by Seeger and Kenyon (executives at Security Trust Corp.), the civil settlement by CIBC, and new information regarding the case, provided grounds to dismiss the charges. In addition, civil charges brought by the SEC were dropped in August 2006.

The dismissal was seized upon by Mr. Spitzer's critics as another sign that he was retreating from prosecutions to focus his time and energy on capturing the Democratic nomination for the governor's seat. It also provided ammunition to critics who claimed that Spitzer was more interested in generating headlines than in carefully building cases. "A prosecutor is allowed and indeed ethically obligated to drop a case if he or she no longer believes it is justified under the law or the evidence," said Evan Barr, a former federal prosecutor in the United States attorney office in Manhattan. "But this decision begs the question of whether the attorney general's office conducted a sufficiently fair and thorough investigation of Flynn's potential defense prior to arresting and indicting him." Others suggested that the Sihpol case affected Spitzer's decision in pursuing actions against Flynn. "It's hard to say if the Sihpol case had any impact," said Robert A. Mintz, a former federal prosecutor. "It's certainly not unreasonable to conclude that the A.G.'s office was looking long and hard at this case to avoid a back-to-back embarrassing defeat" (Anderson, 11/22/05).

SEC Criminal Referrals

In August 2006 former Prudential employee Skifter Ajro pleaded guilty to four counts of securities fraud and four counts of wire fraud. He received two years probation and a $2,000 fine. His former boss Martin J. Druffner pleaded guilty to the same charges in September 2006. He received six months home confinement, in addition to three years probation and a $4,000 fine. The pair also faced a ban from the associating with the securities industry (SEC, 7/18/11). These cases represented two of the few criminal prosecutions that resulted from an SEC referral.

Large Cases, Collaboration, Trends, and Fee Reductions

When looking at the cases resolved by Eliot Spitzer's office, there are three elements that stand out: the relatively large size of settlements compared to other mutual fund cases, the common use of collaboration to investigate and settle cases, and the inclusion of fee reductions as part of sanctions levied against offenders. These elements do not include any factors created by legal or jurisdictional differences between regulatory groups. For example, this section does not discuss why Spitzer brought criminal cases without collaboration from the SEC, as the SEC is only allowed to bring civil cases. It also does not examine why Spitzer's sanctions were, on average, much more punitive than those of the NASD/FINRA. The NASD/FINRA only has jurisdiction over brokerage firms, which generally, were only cases of supervisory failures related to market timing and generated the least profits from the illicit activities.

Spitzer and the Big Cases

Among those organizations most severely punished, there are few apparent commonalities. One factor that does stand out is large fee reductions included among their sanctions. This is true for seven of the top ten most penalized, and there were no fee reductions for any organization that fell below the median punishment of $20,000,000. Logically, including large fee reductions increased the total punishment, pushing that organization higher up the list. However, only Spitzer enforced fee reductions as part of a punishment, so Spitzer was commonly involved in negotiating settlements with the most heavily punished organizations. In fact, Spitzer was only involved in one case with a total punishment below the median. Fee reductions became Spitzer's trademark. As part of the plea deals his office negotiated, he often forced companies to reduce their fees for a five-year period. Spitzer viewed fee reductions as being valuable to the consumer, and continued to pursue them as a type of victim compensation. Overall, Spitzer's fee reductions saved consumers an estimated $915 million.

The mean punishment for organizations involved in market timing and/or late trading was $89,507,025, a figure which is skewed by the top three punishments each being almost double that of any other (all in the $600 million dollar range). Nonetheless, nineteen organizations received punishments above the mean, and Spitzer was involved in fifteen of those cases. It is difficult to determine if Spitzer only chose the largest cases or if punishments were larger because Spitzer was involved. Past examples of his work (investment banking scandal, AIG settlement, NYSE/Grasso settlement) demonstrate that he often was able to extract larger settlements from offenders (Hakim & Rashbaum, 3/10/08).

Supreme Court Rules on Fees

The Supreme Court addressed the issue of fee reductions in the term prior to the Janus decision. On March 30, 2010, in the case of Jones v. Harris Associates, the Court ruled that an excessive fee is not a breach of fiduciary duty unless that fee is so great that bears no "reasonable relationship to the services rendered and could not have been the product of arm's length bargaining" (Vicini, 3/30/2010). Justice Alito wrote the unanimous decision for the Court, adopting a 1982 2nd Circuit decision that created the 'Gartenberg standard' of a reasonable relationship between fees and services rendered and was created by real bargaining. This standard first appeared in *Gartenberg v. Merrill Lynch Asset Management, Inc.,* 694 F.2d 923 (2d Cir. 1982).

The case was initially brought by three investors who used Harris Associates to manage their mutual funds, but discovered that Harris Associates was charging them twice as much as they were charging institutional investors for similar services. The investors also alleged that Harris Associates Board of Directors was not adequately independent when it determined the company's fee structure (Zweig, 8/15/2009). While the Supreme Court's decision is seen as a blow to those looking to lower mutual fund fees, the case could have resulted in higher mutual fund fees if the Supreme Court had also thrown out the Gartenberg Standard. It should also be noted that even in light of the Court's ruling; the settlements reached with Spitzer are not likely to be affected.

Spitzer and Collaboration

While many mutual fund cases achieved similar results (Spitzer's office, the SEC, and NASD joined together to levy fines, disgorgements, and/or professional sanctions for those involved), Spitzer's cases were slightly different, both in the settlements he reached, and in the other parties he involved. Spitzer joined with other state Attorney Generals, or their equivalent, to prosecute several mutual fund cases (see Appendix 4). In eight instances of Spitzer's twenty cases, state offices from Colorado, New Hampshire, Vermont, Kansas, Connecticut, Illinois, Wisconsin, and Massachusetts, joined with Spitzer's office to prosecute an organization involved in the mutual fund scandal. However, only four of the remaining forty-two cases featured a state regulatory organization paired with the SEC, NASD/FINRA, or NYSE to settle a case without the presence of the New York Attorney General's office.

Outside of the Canary Capital case, all of Spitzer's mutual fund prosecutions were done in collaboration with the SEC and NASD, among other agencies. Despite the joint settlements an animosity between Spitzer and the regulatory agencies remained. Statements from Spitzer indicated that he believed the SEC was "asleep at the switch", while the SEC generally avoided public criticism for Spitzer's actions. The one exception came when an SEC representative was asked about some of Spitzer's demands in mutual fund case settlements.

> The Commission's settlement does not require Alliance Capital to offer fee discounts to its mutual fund customers. We determined - unanimously - that such relief would not serve our law enforcement objectives in this case. There were no allegations that Alliance Capital's mutual fund fees were illegally high. This is a case about illegal market timing, not fees. Therefore, we see no legitimate basis for the Commission to act as a "rate-setter" and determine how much mutual fund customers should pay for the services they receive in the future from Alliance Capital. This decision is better left to informed consumers, independent and vigorous mutual fund boards, and the free market. Mandatory fee discounts would (i) require that customers do business with Alliance in order to receive the benefits of the discounts, and (ii) provide monetary relief to customers who were not harmed by the violations set forth in the order. That is why our efforts focused on providing full compensation to harmed investors and a significant upfront penalty (SEC, 12/18/03).

This statement came after the first collaborative case by the SEC and Spitzer's office. It is not clear whether there was a question that prompted this statement, but it was clearly aimed at actions by Spitzer. By directly addressing Spitzer's fee reductions, it attempts to re-frame the debate over how to redress mutual fund harms and also the role of regulatory agencies. The SEC paints the New York Attorney General's office as an activist regulator with their own agenda, while the SEC is portrayed as maintaining itself within the narrow confines of its responsibilities. This action is reminiscent of the multi-dimensionality of power argument made by Goetz (1997). While Goetz' example discusses how actions are classified, this instance has to do with the scope of powers available to regulatory agencies. If certain actions are deemed, by regulatory agencies or others, inappropriate remedies, then the scope and autonomy of the regulatory agency is compromised, as is its ability to address larger wrongs outside of the narrow scope of the immediate problem. Therefore, the potential actions of the regulatory agency are limited before they even have a chance to react to some wrongdoing.

Trends of Penalties over Time

Calavita and Pontell's analysis of the savings and loan prosecutions found that aggressive punishment of "thrift" offenders diminished over time. The first offenders to be tried or settle their cases received harsher penalties than later cases (Calavita & Pontell, 1994). They attributed this trend to state theories of punishment, in which cases went from deterrence to management and protection of politically important actors that were involved in the illegal activities.

In this scandal, trends of decreasing punishment are not as discernible. This may come from the simple fact that there were fewer cases (62 as opposed to the hundreds of cases in the Savings and Loan scandal). In addition, more cases were handled by regulatory agencies or state agencies, in civil courts, and fewer criminal cases. This allowed for more consistent punishment, as a formula for fines and disgorgement had been created by the SEC, and federal oversight required that this formula be applied consistently. In support of this notion, the greatest cause of variation in penalties applied came from Spitzer's requirement of fee reductions. This was one area that was completely outside of the standard punishment formula and did not involve regulatory agencies at all. In fact, the regulatory agencies publicly disapproved of including fee reductions in the settlements (SEC, 12/18/03).

Differences between punishments from agencies are discernible through use of a scatter plot graph (see Appendix 5). From this graph it is obvious that the cases involving Eliot Spitzer and the New York Attorney General's office generally received harsher penalties than those cases in which he was not involved. It should be noted that every case which featured Eliot Spitzer's office also included the SEC. Other state and federal agencies were sometimes involved with Eliot Spitzer, but the SEC was the only consistent entity, except in the Canary Capital case-the initial case of the mutual fund scandal-which Spitzer's office handled alone.

Due to the limited number of cases that comprise the market timing and late trading scandal, possible effects or trends are magnified by dividing this population of cases into sample populations based upon who prosecuted the case. Nonetheless, the group does divide fairly evenly with twenty cases attributable to Spitzer, nineteen to the SEC, and twenty-one to the NASD/FINRA. The Spitzer case penalties averaged $185,077,250; the SEC cases averaged $50,828,053; and the NASD/FINRA averaged $1,393,175. As mentioned above, some of these discrepancies are associated with fee reductions which Spitzer imposed in almost all of his cases. The difference in the SEC and NASD penalties likely reflect the jurisdictional and resource differences also discussed above.

While mean sanctions are informative in comparing the quantity of monetary punishment inflicted by various agencies and organizations, another valuable statistic is the regression line for these cases (see Appendices 5 and 6). This gives an indication of the average case settlements over time, the unit of analysis for Pontell and Calavita. In this study, Spitzer's settlements show a relatively steep decline over time at a rate of $5,346,768 for every month after the initial Canary Capital case was settled in September 2003. This statistic is interesting, although a bit deceiving, as the initial Canary Capital case represented a $40 million dollar settlement, followed by a $600 million dollar settlement three months later, followed by $540 million and $140 million dollar settlements six months after the initial case. Nonetheless, Spitzer's twenty cases did demonstrate this steep decline. SEC cases also showed a much more gradual decline, with a negative slope of $381,238 dollars for every month after the initial settlement. This statistic comes with caveats as well. In the SEC's case, they were not even aware of investigations into market timing and late trading when Spitzer made his announcement of the settlement with Canary Capital. Their first market timing and late trading settlement did not come until March 2004, six months after the Canary settlement a fact which impacts the calculation of their regression line. The NASD/FINRA settlements have the same disadvantageous late start in prosecuting market timing and late trading cases. Despite this, their slope maintained a slightly positive bent, increasing an average of $46,686 per month after the Canary settlement. However, it should be noted that even with a slightly positive slope over the twenty-one cases, the range of NASD/FINRA settlements was much smaller relative to that of the SEC or Spitzer cases, with the highest settlement being $5 million and the lowest $100,000. The Spitzer cases ranged from $600 million to $4,200,000, while the SEC cases varied between $250 million and $350,000.

These results add a nuance to Pontell and Calavita's (1995) findings that penalties decreased over time as a result of defendants being politically involved or connected. In these cases politically connected defendants were punished for their involvement. The difference in this scandal is that even though there was punishment, there was also a possible show of leniency or bias, as federal level regulators did not sanction the politically connected offenders. Instead, these offenders were penalized by self-regulatory organizations and state regulatory agencies, or they sanctioned themselves by firing employees. This demonstrates a possible form of bias as described by Goetz (1997) in his piece on arson as white-collar crime. As Goetz explains, there are multiple forms of bias which are exercised by powerful members of the criminal justice that may represent leniency to certain members or classes of defendants. The traditional form is commonly understood, and it is represented, in white-collar crime cases, through lesser sentences for white-collar crimes versus non-white-collar crimes. The second and third forms of bias are less commonly understood and they are expressed through treatment of the offender outside of traditional sanctions. In this case, as in Goetz's example of arsonists, we observe bias by not allowing the offense to be labeled "crime" so that an offender is not considered criminal. This was demonstrated in market timing and late trading cases when federal agencies did not push for formal charges against UBS and Merril Lynch. Although it is difficult to know how much bias was expressed in the Merill Lynch case, as no agency pushed for formal sanctions, the UBS case is quantifiable because state and self-regulatory organizations issued a total penalty of $50,500,000 and UBS fired two people. Federal regulators, by choosing not to elevate their investigation into charges, would not have attached an "offender" label. The Merrill case is more ambiguous as all sanctions were self-imposed, so, except for a few one line mentions in news reports, no offender label was attached to them through any regulatory agencies or media outlets.

Alliance Capital Management

Alliance Capital Management incurred the largest penalty with a $600 million penalty. The $600 million penalty was unusual in that part of it was reached through regulatory collaboration between the SEC and Spitzer's office, and part was negotiated solely through Spitzer's office.

Both regulatory parties agreed with a $100 million fine against Alliance and $150 million in disgorgement. However, Spitzer's office negotiated an additional $350 million penalty in the form of 20% fee reductions for the next five years, because they have said Alliance charged small investors two to three times as much in fees than their institutional counterparts. This fee reduction is estimated to cost Alliance $70 million annually. The SEC determined-unanimously-that such relief would not serve their law enforcement objectives. Spitzer responded that, "The SEC deal 'sells investors short' (MSNBC, 12/19/03)." This highlights some of the differences that divided the SEC and Spitzer's office since the beginning of the mutual fund inquiry.

Fee Reductions

A critical issue to evolve from the market timing and late trading scandal is the gap between management fees paid by individuals versus those paid by institutional investors. Fund companies often charge individuals at least a quarter of a percentage point more than they charge institutions, Spitzer testified to Congress, in 2003. While this amount may seem small on an absolute scale, the difference is better understood when put into context. Management fees are usually under two percentage points, and may be closer to one and a half points or less. This means that individual customers were being charged 12% to 20% more than institutional investors. Eliot Spitzer tried to narrow that gap by demanding fee cuts in several of his settlements. Other private attorneys followed his lead and began filing suits in civil court, challenging the gap between what is paid by institutions and individuals. (Atlas, 8/26/04).

> As I stated in my testimony to the Senate Banking Committee four weeks ago: "Improper trading and the exorbitant fees charged are both consequences of a governance structure that permitted managers to enrich themselves at the expense of investors... As regulators and lawmakers, our duty to investors is to investigate every manifestation of that breach and to return to investors any and all fees that were improper or inappropriate...The desire for increased fees led managers and directors to abandon their duty to investors and to condone improper and illegal activity. Common sense demands that we at least inquire whether the desire for

increased fees also resulted in fee agreements and charges that were improper" (SEC, 12/18/03).

Spitzer believed that including fee reductions in settlements further redressed harm from market timing by requiring organizations to disgorge the management fees it received for those periods during which market timing was permitted (SEC, 12/18/03). Over the eighteen cases that he settled, twelve included fee reductions as part of their agreement. There were two more cases which included fee reductions, but were settled by Andrew Cuomo in January 2007, the first month that Cuomo was attorney general of New York and Spitzer was Governor. These fourteen cases resulted in over $1 billion in estimated fee reductions, with the largest single case being a $350 million fee reduction from Alliance Capital and the smallest being $5 million which was issued to each of Fred Alger & Company and Richie Capital. The estimated value of fee reductions from the mutual fund cases represented almost 20% of the total penalties levied (see Appendix 7).

Many of Spitzer's critics supposed that the mutual fund scandal, like Spitzer's other white collar prosecutions, were part of a larger plan to gain attention and notoriety towards political ambitions. In that instance, one would expect a pattern to emerge among those institutions sanctioned by Spitzer; especially those cases were there were fee reductions as this was the most populist feature of Spitzer's settlements. Fee reductions reduced the average investor's cost to enter the game, and sought to level the playing field against favored institutional investors. By examining the fourteen institutions that agreed to fee reductions, there is little to tie them together. All the aforementioned institutions were either investment advisers or fund complexes, or both. The only group not included was hedge funds, which is to be expected. Hedge funds would not have a differentiated fee structure for common investors, as they cater exclusively to high level investors. There was no consistency in the nature of offense or the complicity of the organization. Of the fourteen fee reduction cases, there were organizations where many members within the organization took part in the illegal activity, while a few cases saw illegalities driven by a single owner, or small group of managers.

While much is made of timing, relative to publicity and how stories "play" in the media, there does not appear to be a relationship between when an institution was sanctioned and how they were sanctioned. Alliance Capital, the first company sanctioned after Canary Capital, agreed to fee reductions, as did Waddell & Reed, the last organization sanctioned by Spitzer, thirty-four months after the Canary Capital settlement. In fact, the first two companies sanctioned by Spitzer's predecessor, Andrew Cuomo – the same month Spitzer ascended to Governor of New York – included fee reductions. It is possible that these two settlements, with Deutsche Bank and Fred Alger & Company, were largely arranged by Spitzer. The other two, Richie Capital and Hartford, took place six months later. Spitzer's critics may have suspected that only the most prominent defendants would receive fee reductions, as these cases most likely to make headlines. It is true that groups like Bank of America, Janus, and other well known entities were forced to reduce their fees, but so did the Federated Securities Company and RS Investment Management.

Disagreements between SEC and Spitzer

As described earlier in this chapter, Spitzer and the SEC had created a bit of a rivalry during the stock analyst scandal when Spitzer brought the cases unilaterally without seeking out assistance from the SEC despite the nature of the analyst violations. His statements reveal a frustration with the SEC not being as aggressive or punitive as he believed necessary. "My attitude is shame on the OCC, SEC, FDIC, and Wall Street titans, who permitted this debacle…I had a rather acrimonious relationship with the SEC, because I said that they are failing in their fundamental obligation to protect the sanctity of the marketplace (BBC, 11/14/09)." The mutual fund scandal exacerbated those tensions, as it was, first, another example of Spitzer striking out on his own into SEC jurisdiction. Second, mandating fee reductions took headlines away from the SEC as they sought to include themselves in the mutual fund investigations. Spitzer appears to purposefully take jabs at the SEC as he discussed their proposed settlement package.

> The SEC chose not to accept a portion of the Alliance settlement, including fee reductions and an obligation on the Alliance fund directors to publicly establish the propriety of their management fee contracts. That is the SEC's prerogative. However, the SEC's statement that "this is a case about illegal market timing, not fees" reveals a fundamental misunderstanding of the root cause of the harm to

> investors…The SEC is wrong to believe that such measures
> alone are sufficient to compensate investors for past fee
> overcharges. Funds that permitted their investors to be
> overcharged by affiliated management companies must be
> held financially accountable for that conduct. Requiring them
> to pay back those overcharges is not "rate-setting" but merely
> returning to investors money that they never should have been
> charged in the first place (SEC, 12/18/03).

Elements from these statements about the SEC settlement with Alliance Capital would continue to permeate the rest of the fund scandal, and though Spitzer and the SEC would collaborate on many more market timing and late trading cases, the SEC never advocated for fee reductions and Spitzer rarely relented from including them.

Spitzer's critiques of regulatory agencies have not ended with his absence from a political office. He has continued to call for improved regulation of the financial system, while also offering his views on the current state of affairs. "We are going through, what I call, the regulatory charade where the regulators pretend they did not have the power to prevent the crisis we are going through [sic]. The fact is they did have the power, they just chose not to use it. It was an ideological perspective and a hesitancy to use the power that was at the heart of the problem" (BBC, 11/14/09).

Effects of Fee Reduction

One aspect of fee reductions that may not have been considered by mutual fund insiders or regulators is that the idea would catch on and permeate among the industry. While Spitzer sought to lower fees as a punishment to offending organizations, many executives realized that their industry's reputation had been damaged, and that mutual fund companies had been painted as abusive to regular investors. As such, many fund companies began to voluntarily lower their fees. In 2004, more than 850 mutual funds lowered their management fees, up from 239 in 2003, according to a study by Lipper Inc. The trend continued to 2005, when over 700 funds cut fees. The number of rate cuts in 2004, represented the most in over a decade (Dale, 1/27/05). "The reason for the sharp rise in management-fee cuts is the examination by Eliot Spitzer in 2003," said Kip Price, head of Lipper's global fiduciary review unit, which helps fund boards size up returns and costs. "A light was shone on fees, and then there were cuts" (McDonald, 12/14/05). These rate cuts did not come at a particularly down time for the market, but did coincide with the headlines regarding late trading and market timing.

While offenders cut fees to regain investors' trust, the effects of the market timing and late trading scandal spread beyond the offending organizations. In 2005, for instance, the board of directors at T. Rowe Price Group, Inc. – a fund company not involved in the scandal – lowered fees firm-wide. Other organizations not caught up in the scandal have cut fees, too, including Vanguard Group and Fidelity Investments. "Hopefully this will be a trend," Mr. Spitzer said in an interview. "When we examined fees, we found that many mutual-fund boards weren't fulfilling their obligation to actively negotiate for lower fees on shareholders' behalf" (McDonald, 12/14/05). It was this discovery that justified Spitzer's use of fee reductions, and other firms took notice with preemptive fee reductions of their own.

In fact, Spitzer's actions in the mutual fund industry caused some novel concepts to be introduced. After MFS Investment Management fired their chairman due to his involvement in the mutual fund scandal, Robert Pozen, the new chairman of MFS proposed a way to lower fees. He said that MFS would demand brokerage firms break out research and distribution costs from the commissions they charge its mutual funds for stock trades. (Thomas Jr., 3/16/04). This position challenged his fund company counterparts to directly address the issue of high fees, which emerged from the mutual fund scandal, and recapture some of the lost investor confidence. For many years, brokerage firms charged fund companies a full service price for providing them research reports as well as access to all of their trading desks to help distribute their product. According to a research report by Richard Strauss of Deutsche Bank, 40% of the commission paid by a fund company relates to research, 45% to execution, and the rest goes to third-party research and computer aids (Thomas Jr., 3/16/04). Pozen's proposal would ask for 'execution only' prices, potentially eliminating almost half of the current commission rate (Thomas Jr., 3/16/04). However, Pozen's statement had little value by itself, and, apparently, did not gain traction with enough fund companies that they could put pressure on brokerage firms to lower fees.

Other Groups Discuss Fee Reductions

Government Accountability Office

In 2000, before the mutual fund scandal was discovered, the Government Accountability Office (GAO) wrote a report on mutual fund fees. The report showed that mutual funds had not responded to the theory of economies of scale, which supposes that mutual fund fees as a percentage will decrease, as the number of mutual fund investors increases. The GAO took a sample of fifty-one mutual funds that had over 500% growth from 1990 to 1998. During this same time period only thirty-eight mutual funds in this sample reduced their fees by 10% or more and six funds either did not change, or increased their fees. More specific information on economies of scale was indeterminable because specific information on the costs incurred by mutual fund advisers was not available (GAO, 2000). As a result of this report the GAO recommended that the SEC require mutual fund quarterly statements to include a clear breakdown of how much, in dollars, of the client's investment has gone towards mutual fund fees. It is believed that this would provide transparency for clients, which currently does not exist or is obscured by mutual funds' deliberate manipulation of statements so that the information is present, but is difficult for the average investor to discern because of where or how the information is presented. Currently, there are no federal or SEC regulations which limit how much a mutual fund may charge in operating expenses. Regulations only mandate that mutual funds provide adequate disclosure of their risks and costs (GAO, 2000). The primary concerns about this suggestion were if mutual fund companies could use different methods to calculate these numbers and whether the costs of these calculations were to be borne by the company or by the investor.

Responses by the SEC, NASD/FINRA, and Investment Company Institute (ICI) were included at the end of the report, as each group was given advanced copies to review. Despite the GAO suggestion that additional disclosures with specific dollar amounts would be useful for investors and would encourage price competition among mutual funds, the SEC, NASD/FINRA, and ICI each stated that mutual funds already make sufficient disclosures regarding their fees. The agencies also all questioned the idea that mutual funds compete on the basis of performance rather than competing on price or fees. The ICI suggested that price and fees are a part of performance in that a mutual fund's returns are listed as net returns and already include fund fees (GAO, 2000). Despite these initial protests to the GAO report, the SEC made similar recommendations after conducting their own report in 2001. The SEC report examined mutual fund fees and found pricing trends similar to those identified in the initial GAO report (GAO, 2001).

CHAPTER 4

Federal Regulators and Self-Regulatory Organizations

Regulatory Agencies

The SEC is the primary securities and public companies' regulator in the United States. They were founded as part of the New Deal economic and social reforms, and, at the time, had a much more manageable task. In 1940 fewer public companies existed and far fewer people invested in the stock market, which left minimal responsibilities for the agency. In the sixty years since its inception, the agency has grown, but at a much slower rate than the population they police. This results in an over-matched staff – comprised, primarily of lawyers not economists or finance majors – to try and understand, and stay ahead of, bright, financial minds as they seek to skirt economic rules and regulations.

During this recent period of mutual fund investigations and prosecutions, the SEC underwent several changes. They experienced four different chairmen during this time. During the period of illegal action, Arthur Leavitt was chairman of the SEC. He was known for his tough talk against white-collar crime, although many considered him to be more of a man of words than a man of actions (Gasparino, 2005). Leavitt was succeeded by Harvey Pitt, a long time Wall Street lawyer, who was well connected with the major Wall Street banks. He handled problems quietly without as many formal actions. While he may have actually been more ambitious and better able to accomplish real reform than Leavitt, his quiet nature was perceived as regulatory capture and he was practically forced out of the position. This was partly because of Wall Street backlash after the corporate accounting and investment analyst scandals (Gasparino, 2005).

President George W. Bush nominated William Donaldson to follow Pitt. This left Donaldson to clean up the mess of Enron, WorldCom, and others. However, he was not nominated for his ability to reform, but rather a belief that he would restore the status quo to Wall Street. "All the Bush administration wanted him to do – this 71-year-old pillar of the Wall Street establishment, who, among other things, had spent five years not rocking the boat in the 1990's as the head of the NYSE – was calm everybody down, rebuild morale at the SEC and restore some measure of confidence in both the markets and in the companies who stocks and bonds we all buy and sell" (Nocera, 7/23/05). He surprised his supporters by calling for tough reforms and strong actions against white-collar criminals. On his watch the SEC passed Sarbanes-Oxley and several other measures for financial and economic reform. Donaldson's efforts even earned him respect from regular SEC critics. Eliot Spitzer noted, "He revived an institution that had been failing to address its mandate" (Nocera, 7/23/05). Despite the praise he received for carrying out the SEC's mission, not everyone thought highly of him. Conservatives, inside and outside the agency, thought Donaldson had violated partisanship boundaries. "Mr. Donaldson was viewed by many conservatives as a turncoat because he voted so often with the two Democratic commissioners –and against the two Republicans. The Republican commissioners began writing biting dissents to commission rulings" (Nocera, 7/23/05).

Donaldson was succeeded by Christopher Cox, a former conservative Congressman, who was known for his pro-business stance. By the time he was appointed, the large majority of corporate and financial industry cases had been concluded, and Cox focused on limiting litigiousness against corporations-an issue that he had supported after being a plaintiff in a 1995 shareholder lawsuit (Roane, 4/15/07). It was also on Cox's watch that the most aggressive mutual fund reforms fizzled and died. However, even the conservative stalwart found himself taking strong action against another scandal, as executive backdating of stock options became a front page issue. The SEC responded, bringing dozens of cases against corporations and their executives (Cox, 9/6/06).

With the election of Barack Obama to the White House, Christopher Cox resigned, and a new appointment was made to head the SEC. Mary Schapiro, former head of the NASD/FINRA, was named as the most recent SEC director. This represents the first time in recent history that a current or former regulator was picked to head the chief economic regulatory agency. Because of her experience working in regulatory agencies, she may have an advantage, in terms of transitioning into the position and winning respect from her colleagues. However, she could also face disadvantages, as she comes from an agency that has been critiqued as having failed in its mission. One manager at the Government Accountability Office (GAO) was hopeful that Schapiro would be able to "turn the agency around" and commented that it had been a "mess" up until that point (R. Hillman, personal communication, 6/29/09). Regardless of how she is received, she will face criticism as scandals continue to emerge, including Bernie Madoff's long-running ponzi scheme. Statistics are telling, with twice as many investigations in 2009 under Shapiro versus 2008 and Cox. Fines were also up 35% in 2009 (Pethokoukis, 4/16/10). However, without further information about the type of cases being investigated, it is difficult to tell if these changes represent a new culture or reflect response to the recent mortgage scandal.

Theoretical Understanding

There are many theories used to describe the role and purpose of regulatory agencies. Likewise, there are many different views on how, and to what degree, these agencies should act to protect consumers from predatory actors within the business. Advocacy of a particular theory is often synonymous to one's political affiliation, as economics and regulation are prominent political topics.

Conservatives, traditionally, have favored a free market approach similar to that associated with Nobel laureate economist Milton Friedman (Friedman, 1962). Friedman's original approach has been modernized and used to justify free market approaches to regulation, relying on the "invisible hand" or market discipline to control an individual's ability to commit crimes (Easterbrook & Fischel, 1991). These arguments discount empirical findings of collusion in the Savings & Loan scandal, the Insider Trading Scandals, and the mutual fund scandals. Criminologists have found that policies based on neo-classical economic theories have created crime-facilitative structures while decreasing the likelihood of crime detection (Black, 2005; Pontell, 2004). The market timing and late trading scandal also demonstrated how a lack of transparency and conflicts of interest in fund governance, allowed by free market policies, facilitated crime in mutual funds.

Insight into the SEC

Shapiro found that the SEC's particular intelligence gathering strategies and strategic decision-making, more than anything else, controlled which types of crimes they detected. For example, approximately 95% of offenses detected through market surveillance were either market manipulation or self-dealing cases (Shapiro, 1984, p. 104). This is consistent with the nature of these types of crimes, as they are transactions that leave artifacts to be detected through regulatory observation rather than disclosure or victim reporting. Therefore, if market surveillance was regularly utilized by SEC regulators, it is difficult to infer why market timing and late trading were not detected, as these crimes were premised on self-dealing.

One explanation is that illegal mutual fund trades lacked transparency, which made it difficult for the SEC to identify offending investors, regardless of their intelligence gathering strategy. SEC rule 22c-2 addresses this problem by forcing financial intermediaries to supply mutual fund companies with information regarding which clients are making trades and how often those trades are being made (SEC, 9/30/04).

The SEC's non-discovery of mutual fund offenses, despite their intelligence apparatus, is also explained by the SEC's priorities. In this case, the SEC did not consider mutual funds to be a high risk area and they reduced the quantity and quality of mutual fund audits.

> Prior to September 2003, SEC staff did not examine for market timing abuses or assess company controls over that activity because agency staff (1) viewed market timing as a relatively low-risk area that did not involve per se violations; (2) determined that mutual fund companies had financial incentives to establish effective controls over frequent trading because such trading can reduce fund returns resulting in a loss of business; and (3) were told by company officials that they had designated compliance staff to monitor and control market timing (GAO, 4/05, p. 4)

By focusing on mutual fund managerial decision-making and embezzlement crimes, the SEC missed opportunities to prevent market timing and late trading. This demonstrates that regulatory priorities and understanding of the criminal opportunity structure also affect which types of violations are detected.

By combining a better understanding of the SEC's organization and priorities with other theories of regulation, one can see why the regulatory system has consistently failed. Scholars have identified the issue of "system capacity," which, in the criminal justice context, concerns the justice system's ability to expend the money, time, and other resources to process offenders (Pontell, 1984). With white-collar crime, the term has been adapted as "institutional capacity." It is a combination of environmental and internal organizational constraints, including: legal barriers, resource limitations, failures of inter-organizational coordination and cooperation, and the beliefs and practices of agents themselves, which all work together to either enhance or hinder the ability to discover and deter white-collar criminality (Goetz, 1997; Black, Calavita, & Pontell, 1995; Levi, 1987; Pontell, 1984; Pontell et al., 1994).

The difficulty in completing regulatory responsibilities is exacerbated by limited resources, which prevent the SEC from covering its blind spots. This vicious cycle is not exposed until violations build into large scandals, cause financial catastrophe, and reveal the SEC's vulnerabilities. Once a scandal comes to light, as it did in the mutual fund industry, the SEC is forced to make strategic decisions regarding how to shift resources. The only redress for this situation is to either add more resources, or predict where violations are likely to occur. While the latter is unlikely, there have been charges regarding the former. The SEC had a 125+% budget increase, in the wake of corporate accounting and mutual fund scandals. In 2003 the SEC budget increased over 100% from the previous year, $44 million to $100 million (GAO, 2004). The rapid succession of major financial scandals likely convinced legislators to increase the SEC budget in an effort to better police white-collar crime.

To further complicate institutional capacity issues, Shapiro reported a high turnover rate within the SEC. According to Shapiro, "Many of those I encountered were young, briefly passing through the agency on their way to private practice" (Shapiro, 1984, p. 141). She also noted how cases would regularly last months or years. This implies that turnover could negatively affect SEC investigation and prosecution of cases, as agents actively working cases move on to other careers. This could also cause problems as departing agents' caseloads are distributed to other employees. Training new employees and regaining institutional knowledge takes time and other resources from the agency. The time spent training new employees also causes the agency to effectively operate below its maximum capacity. So, high turnover rates of SEC agents causes disruption to the normal case flow, consumes agency resources through training new employees, and negatively affects the agency's efficiency.

The GAO believes that the SEC suffers from system capacity limitations similar to those described by Pontell (1984), and it suggested that the SEC improve its institutional capacity, in order to better understand threats to investors (GAO, 2005c). These findings, combined with Shapiro's findings, create a negative outlook on the SEC's ability to complete its agency mission. Prominent "non-discoveries" that resulted in major scandals, all within the last decade, corroborate this understanding of the current regulatory landscape.

Repeated Inaction

The SEC's "non-discoveries" include some of the largest frauds in history, cases such as Enron, WorldCom, Adelphia, and dozens of other corporate scandals which were discovered because insiders blew the whistle. The lack of oversight from regulatory organizations provided opportunity for these corporate executives to offend without risk of being detected. In fact, the SEC had not audited Enron for more than three years prior to its implosion from massive fraud (Valdmanis, 10/6/02). The SEC's lax regulatory standards on publicly traded companies offered more fuel for critics, as other scandals were discovered and adjudicated by outside sources.

The mutual fund scandal represents the third major scandal which the SEC failed to detect within the first few years of the twenty-first century. As discussed, market timing and late trading cases were exposed by a former employee who chose to approach Eliot Spitzer rather than the SEC (Elkind, 4/19/04)). Although it should be noted that in the mutual fund scandal, as in other scandals, after the initial discovery, the SEC pro-actively investigated abuses. The SEC also managed to negotiate several large settlements including some of the largest ever reached with the SEC (GAO, 2005c). Nonetheless, whistleblowers' reluctance to approach the primary business regulator is an indication of the SEC's public perception.

Among their other failures there is one oversight that went largely unnoticed. In May 2004 the NASD/FINRA Chairperson Robert Glauber announced that discussions between the SEC and NASD/FINRA led them to form a Mutual Fund Taskforce made up of a "cross-section of broker-dealer and mutual fund companies" (NASD, 5/12/04). The taskforce's purpose was respond to SEC rule proposals and provide suggestions on ways to improve mutual fund disclosure, transparency, and issues surrounding mutual fund fees, in response to the late trading and market timing scandal. It is ironic that three of the twenty representatives included in the mutual fund taskforce came from companies that had been sanctioned as part of the mutual fund scandal. The ultimate irony was that one of the members of the mutual fund taskforce, involved in helping to improve transparency and address issues of excessive fees, was Bernie Madoff's son, Mark D. Madoff, Co-Director of Trading for Bernard L. Madoff Investment Securities LLC (NASD, 5/27/04). This is the same Madoff company that was shut-down and liquidated to pay back victims of a massive ponzi scheme.

This observation indicates that the NASD and SEC, in addition to their failures in not detecting the mutual fund scandal, did not do their homework in assembling a committee, as the SEC had been receiving complaints about Madoff and his company since 2000 (Markopolos, 2009). At that time Harold Markopolos, a portfolio manager at Rampart Investment Management and a competitor of Madoff's hedge fund, was tasked with learning how Madoff was able to be so successful. Instead of identifying investing genius, Markopolos quickly deduced that Bernard L. Madoff Investment Securities LLC was a fraudulent organization. It took Markopolos approximately four hours of going over Madoff's documents and using financial calculations to deduce that Madoff and his investment company were a fraud (McCoy, 2/12/09). Markopolos then spent the next eight years tracking Madoff and his company, as well as writing "countless letters and emails to the SEC" advising them about Madoff's illegal activities (Markopolos, 20009). The problem was that for those eight years no one at the SEC heard the whistle being blown. This is a problem that Markopolos believes stems from a lack of understanding about financial markets and having an excess of employees trained in the law but lacking a solid financial background (Daily Show, 3/8/10).

Internal Procedures

In addition to problems detecting scandals, the SEC has been roundly criticized for a lack of formalized procedures when referring cases to other regulatory agencies. The GAO found that SEC files often had missing or incomplete notes regarding resolutions of the SEC investigations. Specifically, the SEC did not record whether referrals to other agencies were or were not made. Consequently, the report's primary recommendation was that the SEC keeps better, or at least some, records when cases were referred to prosecutors (GAO, 2005b). A degradation of the SEC's record keeping quality may have been expected as the agency's workload has increased dramatically over the past three decades, while their staff has grown at a much slower rate. However, the SEC offered another reason for not keeping better records of their cases. The SEC justified these procedures by saying that formal criminal referral record keeping was too time consuming and not effective (GAO, 2005c). Whether or not this is true, it does hinder others from analyzing the SEC's effectiveness and function.

This practice of justifying decision-making within the SEC is valuable for several reasons. An organization that reviews its decisions and employee performance over a period of time, understands what it does well and where it could improve. It could also serve a legal purpose. The SEC might be liable if it were discovered that white-collar offenders are recidivating while the SEC could have prevented this. If the agency took no prior action, it may be legally relevant to know the SEC's justification for non-action.

SEC Punishments

Examining the number of cases that were prosecuted and large sums that were extracted in fines and disgorgements is valuable to understanding how much value the SEC placed on these cases – at least after they had been discovered. Shapiro commented that she had been very impressed by the amount of in-depth discussion that took place among SEC managers regarding enforcement recommendations (Shapiro, 1984, pp. 151-152). Assuming this is still the case, the SEC must have ultimately considered market timing and late trading cases to be important. The other possibility is that the SEC viewed these cases as important to public perception, and the agency did not want to further lose public confidence.

Regardless of why the SEC placed importance on mutual fund cases, it is evident that they did make mutual fund cases a priority and that is demonstrated by the quality and quantity of punishments issued. Penalties ranged from $2 million to $140 million, and averaged $56 million. Enforcement actions were brought against 109 individuals, and the SEC obtained industry bans in all of these cases and fines and disgorgements in some. Settlements ranged from $40k to $30 million. In fact, the three highest penalties were $30 million and two for $20 million each. These cases represented three of the four highest penalties obtained from individuals in SEC history, at that time (GAO, 2005c).

The mean punishment for organizations involved in market timing and/or late trading was $89,507,025, a figure skewed by the top three punishments each being almost double that of the fourth largest punishment (see Appendix 3). Nonetheless, nineteen organizations received punishments above the mean; Spitzer was involved in fifteen of those cases. Of the bottom twenty-two cases, the NASD/FINRA was the sole regulatory body for twenty of them, with fourteen settlements under $1 million dollars. These groups represent opposites in terms of their jurisdictional boundaries and goals. Because of the Martin Act, Spitzer essentially eliminated his jurisdictional restraints and focused on large cases that would make headlines and send a powerful message, while the SEC was involved in both large and small cases. The NASD/FINRA is bounded, as an SRO, to adjudicating broker-dealers only and would be alone in those cases that the SEC deemed too insignificant to join in the investigation and settlement.

Trends of Penalties over Time

Over the course of the market timing and late trading scandal, trends of decreasing punishment are difficult to discern. This may come from the simple fact that there were only sixty-two mutual fund cases. Nonetheless, differences between different agencies' sanctions are clearer through use of a scatter plot graph (see Appendix 5). From the graph it is obvious that the cases involving Eliot Spitzer and the New York Attorney General's office generally received harsher penalties than those cases in which he was not involved. While this piece of information is important, it brings light to another issue. The SEC was involved in every case Spitzer handled, with the exception of the initial case, Canary Capital. Other state and federal agencies were sometimes involved with Eliot Spitzer, but, despite their public feud, the SEC was a consistent partner.

Seven of the eight cases handled by the SEC alone came in well under the mean punishment, with fines and disgorgements ranging from $50 million to just under $3.5 million. However, they did have one case, against Security Brokerage, Inc., which resulted in total penalties over $150 million. Due to the SEC's penalty formula being applied in these cases, it appears as though sanctions in these cases hinged on the amount of offenses that took place and the offender's illicit profit. In total, the SEC was involved in nineteen cases as the sole regulator and the NASD/FINRA was involved in twenty-one. The SEC cases averaged $50,828,053; and the NASD/FINRA averaged $1,393,175. The difference in the SEC and NASD penalties likely reflect the jurisdictional and resource differences previously discussed.

While mean sanctions are informative in comparing the quantity of monetary punishment inflicted by various agencies and organizations, another valuable statistic is the regression line for these cases (see Appendices 5 and 6). SEC cases showed a gradual decline, with a negative slope of $381,238 dollars for every month after the initial settlement. This statistic comes with caveats, however. The SEC was not even aware of an investigation into market timing and late trading when Spitzer announced the settlement with Canary Capital. Their first market timing and late trading settlement did not come until November 2004, three months after the Canary settlement-which impacts the calculation of their regression line. The NASD/FINRA settlements also have the same disadvantageous late start in prosecuting market timing and late trading cases. Despite this, the NASD/FINRA slope was slightly positive, increasing an average of $46,686 per month after the Canary settlement. However, it should be noted that even with a slightly positive slope over the 21 cases, the range of NASD/FINRA settlements was much smaller relative to that of the SEC or Spitzer cases, with the highest settlement being $5 million and the lowest $100,000. The SEC settlements varied between $250 million and $350,000 (see Appendix 6).

Calculating Penalties

The GAO found that the SEC used a formula for determining penalties that was consistent with other cases against investment advisers. They also found that the agency coordinated these actions and sanctions with interested state regulatory agencies. The SEC established a three-tiered system of punishment for offenders. The first tier is $65,000 for organizations and $6,500 for individuals per violation, the second tier is $325,000 for organizations and $65,000 for individuals per violation and the third tier is $650,000 for organizations and $130,000 for individuals per violation (GAO, 2005b). The severity of SEC penalties in mutual fund cases is directly related to this scale. The SEC Director of Enforcement specifically mentioned that the relatively high penalties in mutual fund cases are part of an effort to increase accountability and enhance deterrence in the securities industry. Despite higher penalties, the SEC did not necessarily follow maximum penalty guidelines. If the SEC had imposed the maximum possible penalty, the number of violations discovered would have pushed fines into the billions of dollars. The SEC did not seek maximum penalties because they perceived relatively little harm done to investors and a lack of full awareness by the offenders. SEC staff also believed that advocating a maximum penalty would have eliminated the ability to settle cases, not to mention the likelihood that a judge would have considered the proposed penalty disproportionate for the crime.

The SEC used their discretion in a manner consistent with modern white-collar criminologists. Braithwaite, Geis, and other scholars questioned the wisdom of abandoning deterrence and rehabilitation in regard to white-collar offenses. They believed that white-collar crimes are more rational and, therefore, are better controlled by deterrence and its utilitarian assumptions. White-collar offenders typically have more to lose through criminal conviction or informal means of stigmatization (e.g., respectability, money, a job, a comfortable home and family life) (Braithwaite, 1982; Braithwaite & Geis, 1982; Chambliss, 1967). Therefore, less punitive measures are believed to adequately deter white collar offenders from further crimes.

Tension between Spitzer and the Other Agencies

Some of the tension between Spitzer and the SEC, as identified in the previous chapter, came from fee reductions which Spitzer included in many of his settlements. However, the discord between the two groups went beyond settlement terms. Spitzer may have despised the SEC before he became New York's Attorney General; however, their dislike became mutual with the stock analyst scandal. That was the first time Spitzer utilized the Martin Act to claim jurisdiction over Wall Street, upstaging the SEC. During that period, his non-cooperative approach to regulation and brazen attitude angered several top officials, including then Director, Harvey Pitt (Gasparino, 2005). A perceived lack of effort from the SEC led Spitzer to believe that the SEC was submissive to Wall Street and its political influence. One news source summarized the disagreement as such, "Arthur Levitt has said the pressure from Congress has kept the SEC off Wall Street's back, and Attorney General Spitzer has said the SEC has cow-towed to Capitol Hill" (PBS, 11/26/03).

The feud between the two regulators continued into the mutual fund scandal, as Spitzer again broke the scandal without first informing the SEC. The Former SEC Director William Donaldson admitted that he learned about the late trading and market timing scandal and the Canary Capital case the same way the rest of the public did, through Eliot Spitzer's press conference (Elkind, 4/19/04). Again, Spitzer did not hide his disdain for how the SEC was doing their job. He openly commented on their ineffectiveness, as he quipped at a conference attended by several former SEC officials, "I wouldn't let the SEC lawyers do a house closing for me" (Gasparino, 2005, p. 312).

The SEC did not take this criticism lying down. They admitted being caught by surprise when Spitzer broke the mutual fund scandal, but they continued to defend their investigations and settlements. When Spitzer publicly stated that the SEC had been too lenient with Putnam, Director Donaldson shot back,

> Well, he's wrong on that...We went in and we got a settlement with them, which will get the monies that were involved. The reason we settled with them was to try and prevent the continuation of these practices for the shareholders that are still in those Putnam funds. What we didn't do is close the door on further investigations that we have under way...We cannot put people in jail, we are a civil agency. So the most we can do is to bring sanctions, monetary sanctions, to prevent people from becoming officers and directors and so forth. But as far as putting them in jail, Eliot Spitzer has that sort of authority in New York State. We don't (PBS, 11/26/03).

Given these public displays of animosity, it is almost hard to believe that the two regulatory groups cooperated in so many cases. Perhaps Spitzer recognized that, even with their apparent deficiencies, cooperating with the SEC in the mutual fund cases would be better in the long run. The SEC was still the primary regulator for the business and financial communities, and would continue well after Spitzer had moved on to other venues. It was also important that the SEC be included so that they could have an appreciation for the scandal's causes, allowing them to take steps to close off existing loopholes and regulatory blind spots.

SEC Rule-Making Successes and Failures

The SEC and NASD put forth four proposals to address market timing and late trading in mutual funds. The first proposal increased transparency so that brokerage firms must inform the mutual fund which clients are conducting transactions-an effort to control market timing. The second was a proposal to remove conflicts of interest in the fund's governance. The third suggested adding a 2% fee to all short-term mutual fund transactions. A fourth proposal mandated that all mutual fund orders be processed by market close.

While no proposal passed unanimously, and one proposal sparked a bitter feud, all sides knew there would be disagreements even before they began the reform process. The securities industry complained that the proposed rules would make their work more difficult and costly, while regulators argued that previous laws had failed and new laws were needed to prevent future failures. "There's no question that some of the new rules are burdensome. But given the abject failure of the industry to regulate itself, what choice did they give us?" Mr. Spitzer said. In a rare public agreement, Paul F. Roye, director of the SEC's division of investment management, added "You have some people crying that the sky is falling, but there has to be a cost to doing business the right way" (Atlas, 8/26/04). Despite their united front, the SEC proposals saw only a 50% passage rate.

Rule 22c-2

The SEC introduced rule 22c-2 to combat market timing abuses is. The original rule mandated that a redemption fee be imposed upon any mutual fund sale when that mutual fund was held for five business days or less. The fee would not exceed 2% of the total transaction, and the money would go back into the fund to cover trading costs shared by other fund investors. However, after open debate over the rule, several commentators complained to the SEC that a mutual fund's board of directors could best determine their fund's need for a redemption fee. The SEC agreed and modified the rule to give discretion to each board of directors to implement a redemption fee or not. They also included a contingency that allows for individual exemptions from the redemption fee, at the fund's discretion, if the transaction was because of a personal emergency or if the transaction was below a certain dollar amount. Stanford economist Eric Zitzewitz believes that redemption fee is not a viable solution because a 2% fee will only reduce their profits by that small percentage, making it only slightly less profitable to market time (Zitzewitz, 2003). In addition, making the fee optional and allowing for exceptions creates a loophole similar to the one that originally allowed for differential treatment of fund investors.

Another section of the rule 22c-2 allows the mutual fund greater transparency and information about the transactions of mutual fund shareholders, by obligating broker-dealers to share investor and transaction information at the fund's request as well as carrying out fund instructions (e.g., restricting or removing investing privileges). Before this rule, financial intermediaries such as brokerage firms could hold clients' mutual fund investments in the mutual funds in omnibus accounts. This made it difficult for mutual funds to determine exactly which customers were making illegal trades. However, the current rule provides that mutual funds and financial intermediaries enter into a written agreement that the intermediaries provide funds with information on who is making those trades. The financial intermediary must also agree to follow the mutual fund's instructions to restrict or prohibit any shareholder's future purchases or exchanges if the fund identifies that shareholder as having violated the fund's market timing policies. The individual mutual fund can decide whether the information is to be provided on a regular basis or upon request. (SEC, 9/30/04). The SEC passed Rule 22c-2 in September 2006, and made it effective December 4, 2006. It was also the only measure which received near unanimous support.

While there was much more controversy about subsequent mutual fund reforms, rule 22c-2 had its critics too. In this case, the criticism was less about the substance of the rule than its timing. Broker-dealers were concerned that the mandate for increased transparency was being implemented before they could change their processes to collect and distribute the necessary investor information (Levine, 8/22/06). From the criticisms, it is unclear how much time broker-dealers would need to bring themselves into compliance. Regardless, the push-back on this measure was far less than on any other mutual fund reform proposed in the wake of the market timing and late trading scandal.

The 4:00 pm Deadline

In order to combat late trading, several mutual fund industry members have suggested the "hard four" solution, suggesting that all mutual fund orders placed that day must be processed by 4pm EST. Currently, the process involves a broker-dealer receiving the order, it being passed to an intermediary firm that processes the order, and then it is sent along to the mutual fund company later that day. This process only requires that the order be received by the broker-dealer by the 4:00 pm stock market close. The new rule would require the whole order process completed by 4:00 pm. One of the principal criticisms of this regulation comes from Representative Nancy Pelosi from California. Pelosi recognized that having all orders processed by 4:00 pm EST means that her constituents will have a relatively earlier deadline of 1:00 pm Pacific time. Some intermediary firms also suggest that a hard deadline would create an unofficial order deadline of 2:00 pm EST to assure that all orders are processed by the "hard close" deadline (Damato & Burns, 4/5/04, R1). The earlier deadline would not exist for investors that trade directly through the mutual fund, and critics of the law believe this is an unfair advantage for those investors. As an alternative, critics suggest a national clearinghouse that processes all mutual fund orders. They believe that encryption technologies and outside audits to verify an order's validity can eliminate late trading without the drawbacks of the hard close deadline.

The momentum traders – a subset of the market timers – also oppose the hard close deadline. These individuals wait until just before the market closes to place orders based on pre-determined signals. This tends to negatively affect the long-term mutual fund investors because the fund has to buy or sell securities to accommodate these trades. Studies by Zitzewitz (2001) show that momentum trading dilutes mutual fund profits by approximately $500 million per year (Zitzewitz, 2001).

The SEC and the Investment Company Institute are proponents of the hard 4 pm deadline. They believe that passing this law would demonstrate a committed stance against late trading and would create added deterrence for those that might consider the practice (Damato &

Burns, 4/5/04). There is also a question of why it is important that an investor be able to purchase a mutual fund on a particular day. Long-term investors should not care if the trade was made today or tomorrow. Generally, the market does not move significantly from one day to the next. So, over the long term, small changes would not significantly affect the investment. If a person was market timing the mutual fund then they would concerned with which day they purchased the security. Proponents of the legislation have also considered the "smart close," which would set a deadline for orders to be received by mutual funds by 4:00 pm-just like the hard close-but exceptions would be made for later orders that met certain conditions. As a regulatory compliance consultant to fund companies stated, "[Exceptions] will come with a significant amount of new controls" (Damato & Burns, 4/5/04). This seems to indicate that the timing of orders has become a priority for regulation and oversight. The hard close rule was proposed in December 2003 and it still has not been passed, making it unlikely to ever become law.

Despite not becoming active law, the "hard close proposal" would have addressed Needleman and Needleman's elements of a crime facilitative environment by eliminating one of the mutual fund industry's "traditions of commerce" (Needleman & Needleman, 1979). The time-stamping/order ticket process is outdated for the current state of technology. However, the outdated process remains a "tradition of commerce" and the hard close proposal has met with strong resistance from several mutual fund companies. In fact, when the SEC proposed the hard close rule, it received over one thousand letters-nearly ten times the number of letters received regarding the 22c-2 rule. Many of these letters called the hard-close rule an over-reaction to "a few rotten apples" (Fornelli, 9/13/04). Ultimately, the rule did not receive enough support to pass and was never revived.

An Independent Board?

Perhaps the most controversial proposed regulation mandates that a mutual fund's board of directors be led by a chairperson who is not affiliated with the mutual fund in any other capacity. The goal would be to reduce potential conflicts of interest from having a company insider as the person protecting the shareholders' interests. Proponents of the reform include the SEC chief at the time, William Donaldson; the two Democrats on the SEC; and Putnam's independent chairman

John Hill (Solomon & Hechinger, 6/22/04, C1). The proposal has incited a lot of criticism from mutual fund companies. Even former SEC Chairman Harvey Goldschmid acknowledged that requiring independent chairmen is "highly controversial" (Damato & Burns, 4/5/04). Critics point out that mutual fund companies like Fidelity and T. Rowed Price were not found to have been part of the market timing and late trading scandal, despite their senior Board Chair members also managing funds within the company (Solomon & Hechinger, 6/22/04). *The Wall Street Journal* called this proposal an example of 'slap-dash lawmaking' by an agency "red-faced that Mr. Spitzer exposed the late trading violations". The business periodical called the proposal 'arbitrary' and 'without cause', as they questioned its effect on those funds which were not affected by the mutual fund scandal, but do not have independent managers (Burns, 12/28/04).

This criticism has been countered by outside research, "I find that funds that have lower expense ratios and more outside directors have responded more aggressively to the arbitrage issue, implying that fund governance is an important determinant in how and whether funds respond to the arbitrage issue (Zitzewitz, 2003)". A senior mutual fund analyst for the financial publication, *Morningstar* supported the proposal saying, "We can count on one hand the number of instances in which a fund's board has stood up to the adviser and said, in essence, 'you're fired' (Lutton, 3/12/07)." Critics counter that some of the funds involved in the scandal, such as Putnam Investments, already had an independent chairman, but its mutual fund managers were still involved in market timing. In addition to the issue of the independent chairperson, the SEC has considered requiring 75% of the directors of the board to also be independent. Currently, the 1940 Securities Act requires that only 40% of the directors of the board be independent from the fund-management company (Damato & Burns, 4/5/04). The SEC may be considering this to be a fallback position, if the idea of an independent chairman is not accepted.

Both of these measures were proposed by the SEC on January 23, 2004, and were passed by a 3-2 vote on July 27, 2004. The vote had the commission representatives split along party lines with the two Democrats voting for the measure and the two Republicans voting against it. Former SEC chairman, William Donaldson, cast the deciding vote for the proposition (Nocera, 7/23/05). However, the case was brought before the U.S. Court of Appeals for the District of Columbia, and the Court voted unanimously to send the rules back to the SEC to examine the financial impact they would have on mutual fund companies. The ruling was made in June of 2005, and the timing was relevant because Chairman Donaldson was slated to step down from his position at the end of that month. Donaldson was then replaced with conservative Congressman Christopher Cox (Yost, 6/21/05). The SEC attempted to meet the Court's concerns and passed the laws again. However, the same U.S. Court of Appeals again overturned the law in April 2006 (Labaton, 4/8/06). Despite the lack of definitive information on the effects of an independent chairman, frequent criticisms of the measure combined with William Donaldson's resignation made this proposal untenable and it did not pass a third time.

One of the ironies of the SEC's call for mutual fund governance reform is that similar calls were made in 1999, long before anyone had discovered market timing and late trading issues. Four proposals were made, including: fund boards having a majority of independent directors, independent directors being responsible for nominating any new directors, any outside counsel for directors be independent from management, and improving the public information regarding a mutual fund board's independence. In fact, the 1999 proposals changed the percentage requirement of independent board members from 40% to 50% (SEC, 3/22/99). These proposals were composed after a roundtable forum of independent fund directors held at an Investment Company Institute conference in February 1999. In what could only be term 'accidental foreshadowing', Chairman Levitt stated:

> Whether shareholders realize it or not, how directors fulfill their responsibilities directly affects them every day. From negotiating and overseeing fund fees, to monitoring performance, to policing potential conflicts of interest, fund directors should be on the front lines in defense of the shareholder interest. They need to have the tools, the access and the power to faithfully fulfill their legal duty and moral mandate as the shareholder's representative (SEC, 3/22/99).

If these ideals had been aggressively pursued, the SEC may have been able to save four and a half years of market timing and late trading.

To improve oversight in the financial industry, the SEC also mandated that hedge fund advisers register with the agency. Considering the number of hedge funds involved in the mutual fund scandal, it seems logical to hold them accountable to a federal authority. However, this rule adds to the number of SEC audits to be performed, while the agency already suffers from capacity shortages. Exactly how much this addition will affect the SEC's workload is unknown at this point (GAO, 2005d). It is estimated that since this rule was put into place over one thousand hedge fund advisers have registered with the SEC. Despite the capacity issues the SEC may face, the mutual fund scandal proved that there are risks in not registering hedge funds. As William Galvin, the Massachusetts Secretary of State, said, "Letting hedge funds buy shares in mutual funds is like putting a shark in a goldfish tank" (Sloan, 5/9/07).

SEC v. SRO

A 2005 GAO report noted that it is the SEC's responsibility to evaluate SRO examinations for thoroughness, and the SEC plans to increase the amount of SRO reviews that it conducts. This seems ironic, that the SEC routinely failed in its audits of public companies, but believes it can effectively review work from SROs. The current SEC plan calls for 40% of all broker-dealer reviews to be oversight evaluations where the SEC does a secondary review of an SRO exam (GAO, 2005d). Ideally, these types of reviews would serve two purposes, allowing the SEC to examine broker-dealers for possible violations and performing quality checks on the SRO. However, a 1991 GAO report questioned the value of SEC oversight exams, indicating that they offered little information which would improve SRO examinations. Almost fifteen years later the GAO finds many of the same problems with SEC oversight exams identified earlier (GAO, 2005d). In addition, the SEC has not developed a system to track oversight exams, so there is no valid assessment of how well these exams evaluate mutual fund practices.

Despite the difficulties in using SRO examinations as a data source, the SEC often found broker dealer violations while conducting their SRO oversight examinations. In fiscal year 2004, the SEC found 235 broker-dealer violations while conducting 211 SRO oversight exams (GAO, 2005d). The SEC attributed many of these violations to rule changes which may not have been identified by SROs.

In response to these discoveries, the GAO made a series of recommendations for the SEC. First, they advocate that the SEC regularly assess how resources are being allocated relative to the various types of examinations. This includes examining possible gaps in timely examinations or complete risk assessments. Second, they recommend that the SEC assess its methods for conducting SRO oversight examinations, and the wisdom in allocating resources here as opposed to other areas. Third, they advise that the SEC establish policies to create consistency and quality between the various SEC field offices. Finally, they advocate that the SEC electronically track work performed during broker-dealer examinations (GAO, 2005d). The SEC did not give blanket agreement to the GAO report as with past reports, but they did agree to pursue general recommendations made by the GAO. Unfortunately, no change is likely without support from both the SEC and industry participants.

Positive SEC Changes

By 2005 many of the mutual fund scandal participants had been discovered and regulators had settled the majority of cases. In that year the GAO created a report called "Mutual Fund Trading Abuses: Lessons can be Learned from SEC Not Having Detected Violations at an Earlier Stage" in which it investigated the causes of the mutual fund scandal and why other regulatory agencies never identified it. The report assessed changes the SEC made to their mutual fund oversight program to improve mutual fund company operations (GAO, 2005). While the title of the report appears to highlight the SEC's failure to discover mutual fund abuses, the findings indicate that the SEC made good faith efforts to mitigate known risks associated with market timing. The GAO also found that the SEC did not examine for market timing because the SEC classified it as a "low risk" crime since they believed mutual fund companies had financial incentives to establish effective controls.

The SEC refused to acknowledge the threat despite previously published academic papers, articles in the financial press, and an early 2003 direct tip about market timing received by their Boston office about market timing risks in mutual funds. This tip was made by a mutual fund broker working for a Prudential office in Boston who was aware of fund customers market timing mutual funds. The SEC made a cursory inspection and found that the actions in question did not represent a violation of federal securities law (GAO, 2005). However, the tip did show that SEC assumptions about market timing in mutual funds were incorrect, and by not investigating the tip further, the SEC made an error which created lots of bad press for themselves and cost investors money.

In addition to failing to recognize warnings from academia and financial professionals, the SEC also trusted that companies had established "market timing police", which would handle any market timing cases internally. The GAO investigation found that compliance departments had detected risks as early as 1998, but these departments did not feel independent enough to make comments (GAO, 2004). Before the scandal was made public, the SEC also believed that they could adequately assess risks through routine interactions with staff and reviewing relevant documentation alone. The SEC admitted that they were more concerned with examining mutual trading practices and reports to ensure that the fund adviser was not stealing from the funds. The problem with that logic is that previous scandals (e.g., Corporate Accounting and Savings and Loan) had demonstrated that executives are willing to steal from their own companies.

The GAO found that the SEC did not look for market timing in mutual funds because they viewed other forms of financial fraud as higher risk, and they believed that mutual fund companies had sufficient incentives to prevent market timing because of its detrimental effect on a fund's performance. Unfortunately, they were wrong on both counts. The GAO recommended that the SEC begin routine assessments of compliance officers and review compliance reports on a regular basis. The GAO believes that in order for the SEC to conduct a complete, accurate assessment of market risks and internal controls, it is essential that each audit contain interviews with compliance and other staff, reviews of internal audits and other company reports, and even transaction testing so that the auditor can verify statements and claims from the organization. The GAO also felt that a compliance staff must be independent, in order to reduce risk of future mutual fund abuses. In fact, the GAO found that a majority of the eleven mutual fund case settlements that had been published at the time of their report involved companies without independent compliance staffs (GAO, 2004). This lack of independence led to inaction in alerting authorities or challenging company management when they discovered acts of market timing. The SEC agreed with these assessments, and created several steps to strengthen its program of mutual fund oversight.

A subsequent GAO report on the mutual fund scandal titled "management challenges" examined possible weaknesses within the SEC. Specifically, the GAO found that the SEC is underfunded, understaffed, and lacks legal abilities to obtain proper information, do proper reviews, coordinate efforts with other law enforcement agencies, and collect fines (GAO, 2004). All of these factors contribute to their ineffectiveness at identifying and preventing financial crimes and scandals before they occur, or at least before they balloon out of control. As former SEC chairman William Donaldson said,

> We have 350 or so people out there doing inspections in the mutual fund industry. There are 6,000-7,000 mutual funds, and another 6,000 investment advisors, so it's a big area to cover. And this doesn't excuse what's happened. And a further thing would be that the initial insight into what was going on was an illegal collusion between a hedge fund and a mutual fund, and that's when people want to collude and hide it, it's pretty easy to hide (PBS, 11/26/03).

This highlights the SEC's system's capacity issues, demonstrating regulators' workloads at the time the market timing and late trading scandal was discovered.

Some of the problems with the SEC's ability to regulate white-collar offenders come from gaps in its legal authority which can impede the agency's ability to gather information, cooperate with other law enforcement agencies, and collect fines owed by violators. The SEC's director of enforcement told Congress that under current securities' rules, SEC staff is not allowed access to grand jury testimony (GAO, 2004). This requires SEC staff to conduct their own separate investigation, which is likely duplicative to much of the information already gathered by federal or state criminal authorities. The SEC also has no ability to protect privileged information supplied to them through confidential sources. SEC staff believes that this puts them at a disadvantage during an investigation because involved parties have a disincentive to provide protected information to the SEC.

The collection of fines and penalties from offenders is another difficult and inefficient area for the SEC. The agency is often forced to go through long, complicated efforts to enforce settlements and suits. SEC staff has pushed for the ability to contract with private attorneys to conduct litigation and enforce collection orders (GAO, 2004). This problem may be remedied through a Congressional bill which would allow for the SEC to create such contracts to improve their collection process and free more time to focus on investigations.

As part of its examination of the mutual funds scandal the GAO evaluated revisions of the SEC's examination process. In 2004 the SEC had 495 regulators to examine 9,517 mutual fund entities (GAO, 2005d). This was a much larger ratio than any other agency faced. After the mutual fund scandal was discovered, the SEC decided to revise their fund examination process, which was largely supported by SEC staff who did not believe that routine examinations were effective in detecting problems. With a focus on sweep and cause exams, a sample of "lower risk" funds or advisers will be randomly selected for examination every year, with all high risk advisers and funds reviewed every two to three years (GAO, 2005d). The SEC believes that by conducting random sampling of low risk entities they will be able to project violation rates and use this to determine if there are problems among the low risk population. In addition to changing examination patterns the SEC has begun to implement an electronic surveillance system that receives data transmitted from funds and investment advisers. The system will seek out problematic patterns, and identify issues outside of routine examinations.

The problem with this change is that there is no evidence this method will be more effective, or how mutual funds involved in the scandal would have scored on this SEC risk scale. In addition, if lower risk funds are only examined every ten years it will be difficult to assess changes within the fund that may elevate their risk status. This creates an opportunity for low-risk mutual funds to adopt unsafe practices and go undetected for many years. Included in this SEC risk assessment program is a scorecard for mutual funds, which regulators are to use every time they examine a mutual fund. This scorecard is supposed to help the agency determine how that fund should be classified.

Unfortunately, the GAO found missing or incomplete usage of the scorecards in the mutual fund audits they examined. A sample of 546 scorecards completed during 66 routine mutual fund examinations at various SEC field offices, found that only 6% had any evidence of supervisor review, represented by a signature on the scorecard. In addition, 17% of examinations failed to include any scorecards and another 23% had at least one missing scorecard. Of those reports with scorecards, 5% lacked any documented evidence to support claims made on the cards, and 4% of scorecards differed from comments recorded with the examination report (GAO, 2005d). All of these factors display a lack of commitment to eliminating previous discovered shortcomings. The GAO report also revealed that the SEC does not review its examination paperwork, because of limited resources. This finding lowers expectations of improvement in detecting and preventing crimes in the mutual fund industry, and leads one to believe that the SEC's "stream lining" of examinations is really window dressing until the next regulatory failure.

CHAPTER 5
Lessons Learned

The market timing and late trading scandal has provided an opportunity to consider many theories of white-collar crime and regulation. As part of this discussion, the conclusion will break the scandal into three parts: causes, prosecution, and reform, to try and gain a better perspective of how or why each phase occurred, then compare these findings with current understandings of white-collar crime. Each section will discuss findings from this study and their relation to current theory, as well as offer policy suggestions regarding what can be done to prevent events like these from reoccurring. The last section will examine a new regulatory plan proposed under the Obama administration and consider how it addresses some of these regulatory challenges.

Causes of the Scandal

Bad Apples or a Spoiled Bushel?

The "few bad apples" analogy was regularly invoked to explain causes of the various recent scandals. However, few ever questioned its accuracy, or whether it was simply a convenient method of explaining away larger, systemic issues. By blaming the wrongdoing on a few bad actors, interested parties were able to limit negative public reaction. The "bad apple" analogy also eliminates the possibility that the white-collar crime was pervasive. As Goetz discussed arson as white-collar crime, he noted that when officials do not include white-collar crime as a possible label for an action, that label never gets applied and the action is explained as something else (Goetz, 1997).

This is an example of how officials can control 'knowledge' or 'power' over an issue. In the case of market timing and late trading, it would have been impossible to classify it as an accident. Instead, they sought to control how people perceived the scope of the problem. This lead the public to believe that the problem was resolved when those bad actors were caught, and no further investigation or reform would be needed. In reality, the system had been corrupted and opportunities for market timing and late trading continued to exist. By removing those individuals committing market timing and late trading they were simply making room for a new group of market timers and late traders.

Black (2005) used a version of the "bad apple versus spoiled bushel" analogy to help explain systemic problems in the financial and business communities. The difference is that Black utilizes the full phrase, "A few bad apples spoil the bushel." The shortened version, used to minimize the scandal, is supposed to indicate that only a few bad actors were involved in the wrongdoing, and they were identified and cast out of the financial industry bushel. However, that is a misinterpretation of the original meaning. "A few bad apples spoil the bushel," is supposed to suggest that a few bad pieces or actors can corrupt a whole system if these bad pieces are left in contact with good ones. In Black's example from the Savings and Loan scandal he identifies how a few actors were able to pervert incentive structures and weaken regulation, which created motive and opportunity for Savings and Loan owners to steal from their own institutions (Black, 2005). This same problem is also found in the corporate accounting scandals, where proposed incentive structures for success actually created opportunity and motivation for executives to defraud their company and investors.

The market timing and late trading scandal also fits this analogy well. According to Eliot Spitzer, Eddie Stern and a few of his employees at Canary Capital managed to draw in forty to sixty other organizations that might not have been otherwise involved in these practices (Elkind, 4/19/04). The original market timers talked about having to move from mutual fund to mutual fund, as they searched for a fund that would allow them to practice timing without banning them from the mutual fund. By disseminating their unethical trading strategy, the system was corrupted into more egregious illegality. The newer generation of market timers actively sought out illegal arrangements and had other organizations colluding with them.

Leading by Example

Related to this issue of individuals versus systemic causes is the question of how similar practices could appear in different areas of the industry, at roughly the same time. One of the answers is that the financial industry, like much of the business community, is a copycat industry. When a member of their group succeeds, others are eager to learn and mimic those methods so that they may find equal success. This was the reason that Harry Markopolos discovered Bernie Madoff's ponzi scheme before anyone else. His bosses noticed Madoff's success and charged Markopolos with learning Madoff's methodologies, a process which quickly led to Markopolos discovering Madoff's ponzi scheme (Markopolos, 2009). Individual investors are no different than their hedge fund counterparts, as everyone is looking for the secrets of success. That is why there is a market for multiple television channels, shows, magazines, and newspapers dedicated to the financial markets. That is why, when the book *The New Market Wizards* came out in 1992, Eddie Stern was there to learn about market timing (Schwager, 1992). Stern was able to take what he learned from early market timers and adapt their strategies through collusion with fund companies and securities clearing firms, late trading, and increased scale of hedge fund investments combined with his personal wealth.

In many of these cases, illegal practices at the firm were passed down from the organization's leadership. This is consistent with Clinard's findings regarding white-collar crime (Clinard, 1983). As he concluded, top management's opinions consistently determine an organization's level of compliance. This was true in the case of Canary Capital, PBHG, Alliance Capital, Strong Funds, Security Trust, and many others, where top management participated in, or condoned, the offenses. In all of these cases, regulators considered having management involved as an aggravating circumstance of the offense. Regulators punished these executives through heavy fines, criminal charges, or firings and industry bans. Having self-dealing or executive-endorsed cheating creates a problem for the SEC and other regulatory bodies, because the high ratio of mutual funds to regulators requires regulatory agencies to rely upon companies' ability to self-police and detect violations like market timing and late trading. As we saw in the Strong case, management could direct compliance departments away from, or gain their complicity in, the illegal activity (Elkind, 4/19/04). A corrupt compliance department meant that the regulators not only lost their best weapon of prevention, they actually had that weapon turned against them. Now, the compliance department, in addition to not catching illegal trading, made it appear as though everything was legal and proper. This combination of factors represents almost the perfect crime, as it is both potentially endless and virtually undetectable. The only weakness is that the number of people involved in a complex scheme creates many opportunities for an individual to blow the whistle. However, it should be noted that it took over five years before anyone notified authorities to what was happening in the mutual fund industry. Had it not been for Noreen Harrington, Canary Capital, and Eliot Spitzer, it is unclear if these self-dealing executives would have ever been caught.

Behind the Times

Needleman and Needleman's (1979) study of crime-facilitative structures applies to the mutual fund industry, as traditions of commerce made it easier for white-collar offenders to participate in late trading and market timing without detection. Using once a day trading and manual date and time stamping for mutual fund orders is more than simply not utilizing new technologies. It makes it easier for motivated individuals to take advantage of outdated methods for doing business. When Eddie Stern wanted to market time and late trade for Canary Capital, he kept soliciting people to collude with him. He knew he would receive a lot of rejections, but he only needed a few people to agree in order to rig the system in his favor. He found those people, and they were able to easily manipulate outdated manual safeguards and create their opportunity for fraud. If real-time trading were allowed in mutual funds, as is done with stocks, it would be more difficult for brokers to slip in trades executed after the market close.

Final Points

The difficulty in addressing causes of the scandal is that the answer is multi-dimensional and, at best, will only decrease opportunities. While some pieces, like modernization of the trading system, would be relatively simple and straightforward, changing the business community would be more difficult. Equality would have to become a valued trait among executive leadership. As Coleman (1987) and Wheeler (1992) predicted, without a sense of equality firms will continue to compete for the few high-value customers, creating incentives to cheat in order to earn their business. This feature of business rewarded managers who cheated and helped lead to collusion in allowing market timing and late trading, which spread throughout the system to spoil the bushel.

Prosecutorial Approaches

Regulatory Differences

The most obvious difference between the SEC and Spitzer's regulatory actions was Spitzer's inclusion of fee reductions into a number of settlements. While has already discussed at length in chapter three, at issue is a philosophical difference about harm and victim compensation. The SEC believed the penalty should match the offense, and it should redress that specific injury. Spitzer used the offense as an excuse to broadly examine an organization's offenses and rectify all wrongs consumers had suffered related to the offense. In other words, if one were to think of a company's actions like a spider web, the SEC sought to repair the one strand which had been broken. Spitzer repaired that strand, but he also looked for connected strands which had been damaged or weakened and sought to strengthen those as well. Spitzer's approach to justice is more holistic and sought to empower the consumer, rather an address a single grievance.

It was for this reason, along with his willingness to take on large, powerful entities that Noreen Harrington sought out Spitzer when she blew the whistle on Canary Capital. The SEC, given their track record, did not inspire the same confidence. Without an individual like Spitzer in a position such as state attorney general it is unknown where Harrington could have gone to voice her complaint. The willingness to be aggressive and pro-active in their enforcement, even against large corporations, is what separated Spitzer and the federal regulatory organizations. The SEC was active and effective once wrongdoings had been exposed, but were ineffective beginning and executing new investigations.

Moral Entrepreneurs

Immoral leadership in the financial industry was one of the mutual fund scandal's root causes. Therefore, it should not be a surprise that strong, moral leadership led to successful investigatory and prosecutorial outcomes. In chapter three, we saw that the market timing and late trading scandal would likely not have been discovered without the presence of strong leadership like Eliot Spitzer. As an example of Becker's moral entrepreneur, Spitzer vigorously pursued an issue that others had previously ignored. He innovated by using the Martin Act to stretch his jurisdictional authority, so that he could investigate and prosecute market timers and late traders. Then he advocated for tough, industry-wide reforms to prevent the problem from reoccurring.

The strength of Spitzer's leadership is more apparent when contrasted with the SEC's leadership and results. During the period that Spitzer was in office as New York's Attorney General, the SEC went through four directors. Each of these directors had very different styles and approaches to regulation. Leavitt provided a lot of tough talk about enforcement and regulation. He also managed to pass laws creating a higher number of independent members on mutual fund board of directors. However, he provided more rhetoric than effective action inasmuch as a number of major violations and violators continued on his watch. Pitt sought a more cooperative relationship between Wall Street and the SEC (Gasparino, 2005). This was an ideal situation for the Republican majority in Congress and the White House, but was not popular in the face of numerous scandals emerging while he was in charge. His early resignation brought Donaldson, who was supposed to be of the same mold as Pitt. However, Donaldson recognized that the various scandals required a real, tough response that changed those conditions which created the original problems. While Donaldson did not completely satisfy any group, he did manage to earn the respect of non-federal regulators, such as Spitzer and Massachusetts Attorney General William Galvin (Nocera, 7/23/05). Donaldson also had the longest tenure of any of the four directors. This likely allowed him to better instill his agenda and train SEC staff to work towards his vision of the financial regulation. Cox, while not a complete opposite of Donaldson, was more in-line with how Conservative legislators hoped Donaldson would act. The majority of cases emanating from the financial scandals of the early 21st Century were already resolved by the time Cox took office, but he did less to seek out new areas for the SEC to be pro-active (Roane, 4/15/07). These are all prime examples of how the quality of leadership affects an organization's ability to function. Not to mention how frequent turnover at the top – and throughout the organization – can make it difficult to implement a vision, when that vision changes as a new director comes into office every few years.

Final Points

The salient issue from this section, much like the first section of the study, is leadership. In this case, it is leadership among the regulatory community. High turnover rates among the SEC's directors and staff have negatively affected their performance since Shapiro studied them in the 1970's. This may seem contradictory, as Spitzer had only been in office a short time before he started pro-actively prosecuting white-collar offenders. However, the two positions are very different. Spitzer had been a prosecutor before he took over as the state attorney general, and had extensive experience in this type of job. None of the SEC directors had ever worked in a regulatory agency before. In fact, most of them had previously been Wall Street defense lawyers, who battled against the SEC in court. That is what will make Mary Schapiro's tenure as SEC director telling. She is the former head of NASD/FINRA and came into the SEC with regulatory experience. Of course, in addition to experience, one must also contain the quality of moral entrepreneurship that exists independent of professional experience.

Reform and Reaction

Do Reforms Address Causes?

Only two of the original four proposals for mutual fund reform were adopted – even though a third reform passed, but was later challenged in court and repealed. Donaldson was the driving force behind these reforms, and his resignation in June 2005 eliminated any chance of increasing the requirement for independence on a mutual fund's board of directors, or adding a 'hard close' to mutual fund trading. His replacement, Christopher Cox, represented a conservative that followed the party line, and major reforms were not addressed while he was leading the SEC.

Of the two reforms that passed, one of them may make a significant difference in a mutual fund's ability to police illegal trading within its funds. The other will more likely be an annoyance, rather than a hindrance, to illegal traders. Increasing transparency regarding trades in mutual funds was a necessity for improving compliance in this area – as demonstrated in the Prudential case, where over 25,000 letters and emails were written complaining about allowing their clients to market time (Henriques, 12/11/03). Canadian Imperial Bank of Commerce (CIBC) also received over one thousand letters and emails complaining about allowing market timing (Goldstein, 12/2/03). Ironically, because of a lack of transparency, those are just the instances that fund companies could identify. Now that fund companies will have more knowledge of which individuals are making short term trades, they should be able to better police this activity. The test will be whether they enforce their own laws. During the market timing and late trading scandal there were several instances of funds being aware of violators, but condoning their behavior because of quid pro quo arrangements. This new law will at least allow mutual fund companies to identify the wrongdoing, if they chose to utilize this information.

The addition of redemption fees on short term trades appears more as a symbolic measure against market timing than as a practical means of prevention. Stanford economist, Eric Zitzewitz (2003) identified that a 2% redemption penalty for market timers is not likely to hinder this practice when timers are averaging returns over 35%. In addition, the redemption fee is probably as likely to snare innocent individuals making a single, short-term trade than it is to penalize hard-core market timers.   Another point of concern is that this is not a mandated redemption fee for all short-term trades. The regulation only sets a maximum on the amount a fund company can penalize for these trades. The mutual fund companies are free to not incorporate this fee into their internal regulations, and they are also given the power to make exemptions on a case-by-case basis. During the scandal, standard mutual fund policy was that market timers would be banned from trading in that fund. However, some mutual funds were already identifying market timers and making case-by-case exemptions for them. In the end, this regulation will likely have little effect on market timing.

The last proposal, the hard close, would have gone a long way to addressing root causes of the fund scandal, as it eliminates one of the traditions of commerce that continues to exist in the fund industry. A hard close in the mutual fund market would also allow regulators and compliance officers to utilize new technology to prevent future violations. Currently, too much of a gray area exists with mutual fund orders being processed well after the official market close, with an internal, manual time stamp as the only indication that an order was received on time. As with the Bank of America case, Theodore Sihpol III managed to beat the system by having access to a time stamp key. This allowed him to simply open the machine and turn the internal clock back so that the time stamp be faked to look as though the order was received on time (Elkind, 4/19/04). Given the relative ease of beating this system, as well as the inventiveness and demonstrated amount of learning and mimicry that exists in the financial industry, this process needs to be improved.

In the 1940's when the majority of mutual fund regulations were developed, technological limitations necessitated using a manual time stamp. However, technology has advanced significantly in the past seventy years. If companies wanted to, or were mandated to, they could implement an electronic time stamp when the order was received, making it more difficult to legitimate late orders. This issue is closely related to the traditions of commerce which exist in the mutual fund industry, and which are exploited by insiders to perpetuate fraud. Simple modernization of the financial system at regular intervals would not eliminate fraud completely, but it would prevent white-collar criminals from using the same method of fraud for decades. It is common for banks to update technologies to prevent robberies, cheque fraud, or employee embezzlement. So why are financial institutions so hesitant to put in preventative measures against collective embezzlement and white-collar crime by their vice-presidents, presidents, and executive board?

Improving the Theory of Responsive Regulation

While the majority of this chapter has affirmed common theoretical approaches to white-collar crime, there is one theory that this study may be able to improve. Ayres and Braithwaite (1992) developed "responsive regulation" which seeks to have governments or private actors vary their regulatory response based upon the severity of the offense and the likely success of a particular approach (restorative justice, deterrence, or incapacitation). They believe responsive regulation can cover the weaknesses of any one punishment theory, with the strengths of the other two. In order to do this, Ayers and Braithwaite created a "pyramid of regulation" that recommends regulators begin with the least punitive response and move their way up to most punitive, if the act is very serious or if previous punishments have failed (Ayres & Braithwaite, 1992; see Appendix 2). Problems in the mutual fund scandal derived from multiple regulatory agencies overseeing the financial community while lacking a comprehensive view of the industry, including less regulated areas like hedge funds. A layered regulatory system, such as that which Ayres and Braithwaite described, failed because of a general lack of communication and transparency. It is difficult for any agency to truly comprehend the actions of a single financial organization when the regulatory organization does not have a full view of a company's interactions. In order for a system of responsive regulation to function properly, the regulatory bodies must be able to communicate amongst themselves and also have a comprehensive understanding of the various illegal transactions that are occurring between different entities within their given jurisdictions.

Final Points

As with any reform, the outcomes observed over a reasonable amount of time is the only accurate way to tell if it is effective. However, reforms have a better chance to be effective if they address the problem's root causes. In this case, the results are mixed. The two reforms that passed in response to the mutual fund scandal do address causes of the scandal – namely, lack of transparency and profit motive for market timing. While transparency has been improved, the redemption fee does not eliminate the profit motive, but rather only slightly reduces it. Without addressing mutual funds' governance structure or eliminating their traditions of commerce, the reforms have left gaping holes in the industry's ability to maintain preventative regulation.

A New Regulatory Structure?

Finally, before the 2008 election and in the face of the mortgage scandals, candidate Obama pledged to reform the regulatory system to reduce the likelihood of these events reoccurring. While reform has not yet been finalized, there are various proposals being considered. The official regulatory proposal from the Department of Treasury includes creating a 'Financial Services Oversight Council', responsible for identifying firms who might fail and threaten financial stability. They also would act to increase communication between regulatory groups and mediate jurisdictional disputes (Department of Treasury

[DOT], 6/17/09, p. 11). The potential benefit is that an oversight group could eliminate breakdowns in communication that hampered previous investigations. For example, the oversight council may have been able to help Spitzer, the SEC, and the NASD/FINRA better coordinate their settlements and avoid disputes that divided the regulatory groups.

Recently, Congress has made progress towards passing this new regulatory plan. In fact, Treasury Secretary, William Geithner, stated that he believes the regulatory reform bill will pass Congress in 2010 (CBS News, 4/17/10). The plan calls for a new consumer protection agency which will regulate the areas of credit, savings, payment, and other consumer financial products and services. It will also mandate transparency and simplicity in all disclosures and communications with consumers, as well as enforce fair lending laws and ensure that all consumers have access to financial products (DOT, 6/17/09, p. 16). News of this bill's movement through Congress has been announced in conjunction with the SEC civil lawsuit against Goldman Sachs for profiteering from mortgage derivatives which the government claims Goldman Sachs knew were worthless (Pethokoukis, 4/16/10). This lawsuit is interesting, both in that it may indicate this administration understands and appreciates white-collar crime's effect upon the economy, and that the suit was brought by the SEC. After a decade or more of failures, these may be indications that the SEC has returned to relevancy, and signal that events like the market timing and late trading scandal may be prevented in the future.

Appendices

Appendix 1:

Mutual fund transaction:

Investor ⟹ Broker-dealer ⟹ Order-ticket with time-stamp ⟹ Wired to clearing house or handled internally ⟹ Net orders sent to mutual fund

Step 1: The investor places an order with the broker-dealer to buy or sell the mutual fund.

Step 2: The broker-dealer records the order and an order ticket with a time-stamp is created.

Step 3: The order is then wired to a clearinghouse to be processed, or the order is processed within the brokerage firm's clearing division.

Step 4: The net orders are then sent along to the mutual fund company to be processed.

Late trading transaction:

The diagram is the same, but the steps are different… Step 1: The investor places an order with the broker-dealer to buy or sell the mutual fund after the market has closed.

Step 2: The broker-dealer records the order and an order ticket with a fraudulent time-stamp is recorded.

Step 3: If the news is in the investor's favor, the order is then wired to a clearinghouse to be processed, or the order is processed within the brokerage firm's clearing division. If the news is against the investor, then the order is not processed.

Step 4: The net orders are then sent along to the mutual fund company to be processed.

Appendix 2:

Ayres and Braithwaite (1992)
Pyramid of Regulation
License revocation
License Suspension
Criminal Penalty
Civil Penalty
Warning Letter
Persuasion

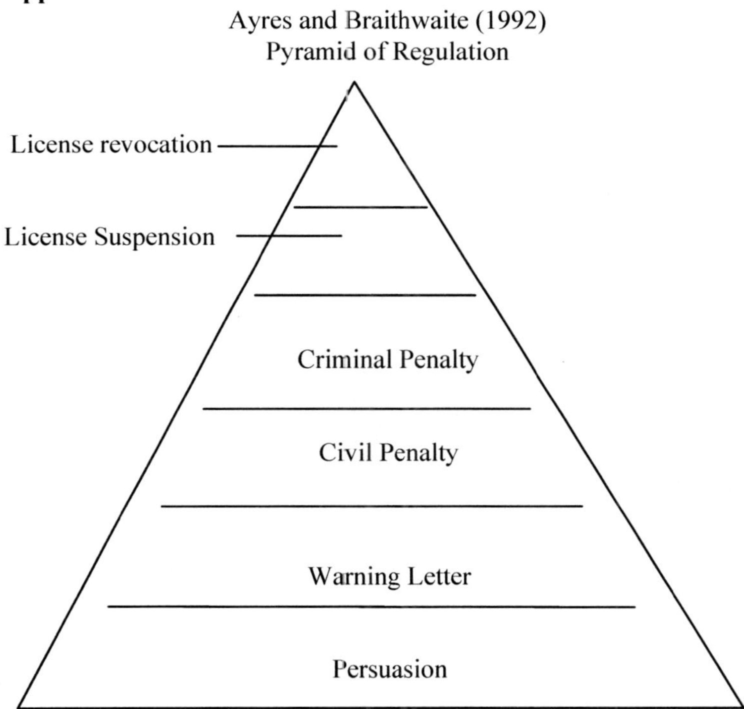

Appendix 3: Offenders & Penalties

Organization	Total Penalties	Individuals Sanctioned
Bank of America	$685,400,000	1
Alliance Capital	$600,000,000	0
Prudential	$600,000,000	14
Invesco Funds Group	$364,340,000	4
MFS Investment Mgmt	$350,500,000	2
PBHG	$260,000,000	2
Bear Stern's clearing division	$250,000,000	3
Janus	$226,200,000	0
Deutsche Bank	$220,130,000	1
Millenium Partners, LLP	$180,575,000	5
Strong Mutual Funds	$175,800,000	3
Security Brokerage, Inc.	$153,000,000	1
Columbia Funds	$140,260,000	3
CIBC	$126,000,000	1
Putnam	$110,000,000	3
Hartford	$110,000,000	0
Federated Securities Company	$100,000,000	0
Banc One Investment Advisers	$90,500,000	1

Organization	Total Penalties	Individuals Sanctioned
AIM Advisors and Distributors	S87,500,000	0
Waddell & Reed	$77,000,000	0
UBS AG	$50,500,000	2
Franklin Templeton Advisers	$50,000,000	0
PIMCO	$50,000,000	0
Smith Barney	$50,000,000	4
Fred Alger & Company	$45,400,000	1
Canary Capital Partners	$40,000,000	1
Ritchie Capital	$40,000,000	0
Veras Hedgefunds	$37,700,000	2
Evergreen Investment	$32,650,000	1
RS Investment Management	$30,300,000	2
Conseco, Inc.	$20,000,000	0
Ameriprise Financial	$17,000,000	0
Zurich Capital Markets	$16,800,000	0
Southwest Securities	$11,275,000	3
Franklin Templeton Advisers	$5,000,000	0
MetLife Securities	$5,000,000	0
Oppenheimer & Co.	$4,500,000	5
Fremont Advisers	$4,200,000	2

Organization	Total Penalties	Individuals Sanctioned
A.G. Edwards	$3,860,000	3
General American Life Insurance	$3,463,000	1
Janney Montgomery Scott	$3,260,000	2
ING Fund Distributors	$2,925,000	1
Diversified Investors Securities	$2,250,000	0
James River Capital Corp.	$2,250,000	1
State Street Research Investment	$1,500,000	0
Sentinel Financial Services	$1,360,000	1
First Allied Securities	$871,500	1
H & R Block	$825,000	0
Kaplan & Co.	$750,000	2
Davenport & Co.	$738,000	0
Jefferson Pilot	$689,000	0
National Securities Corp.	$650,000	2
Rafferty Capital	$410,000	0
Banc One Securities Corp.	$400,000	0
Charles Schwab	$350,000	0
Chase Investment Services	$290,000	0
A.B. Watley	$245,000	4

Organization	Total Penalties	Individuals Sanctioned
TD Waterhouse	$150,000	0
D.A. Davidson & Co.	$150,000	0
Stifel Nicolaus & Co.	$125,000	0
SII Investments	$100,000	0
National Planning Corp.	$100,000	0
Fidelity Investments	$0	16
Security Trust	$0	2
Morgan Stanley DW	$0	2
Merrill Lynch	$0	4
Totals	$5,445,241,500	109

Appendix 4: Offenders and Sanctioning Timeline

Organization	Sanctioning Agency	Months after first case
Canary Capital Partners	NY	0
Alliance Capital	SEC, NY	3
MFS Investment Mgmt	SEC, NY, NH	5
State Street Research Investment	N/F	5
Columbia Funds	SEC, NY	6
Putnam	SEC, MA	7
Strong Mutual Funds	SEC, NY, WI	8
PBHG	SEC, NY	9
Banc One Investment Advisers	N/F, SEC, NY	9
Davenport & Co.	N/F	9
TD Waterhouse	N/F	9
D.A. Davidson & Co.	N/F	9
Stifel Nicolaus & Co.	N/F	9
SII Investments	N/F	9
National Planning Corp.	N/F	9
Invesco Funds Group	SEC, NY	11
Janus	SEC, NY, CO	11
Franklin Templeton Advisers	SEC	11
Conseco, Inc.	SEC, NY	11

Organization	Sanctioning Agency	Months after first case
National Securities Corp.	N/F	11
PIMCO	SEC	12
Charles Schwab	SEC, NYSE	12
AIM Advisors and Distributors	SEC, CO, NY	13
RS Investment Management	SEC, NY	13
Sentinel Financial Services	N/F	13
Fremont Advisers	SEC, NY	14
H & R Block	N/F	15
Kaplan & Co.	SEC, NY	16
Southwest Securities	N/F, SEC	16
Banc One Securities Corp.	N/F	16
Jefferson Pilot	N/F	18
CIBC	SEC, NY	22
Janney Montgomery Scott	N/F	25
ING Fund Distributors	N/F	25
First Allied Securities	N/F	25
Federated Securities Company	SEC, NY	26
Millenium Partners, LLP	SEC, NY	27
Veras Hedgefunds	SEC, NY	27

Organization	Sanctioning Agency	Months after first case
Ameriprise Financial	SEC, MN	27
Chase Investment Services	N/F	27
Security Brokerage, Inc.	SEC	28
UBS AG	NYSE, NJ	28
Diversified Investors Securities	N/F	29
Bear Stern's Clearing Division	SEC, NYSE	30
Waddell & Reed	SEC, KS, NY	34
Prudential	N/F, SEC, NJ, MA, NY	35
MetLife Securities	N/F	36
James River Capital Corp.	N/F	37
Fred Alger & Company	SEC, NY*	40
Deutsche Bank	SEC, NYSE, IL, NY*	40
Zurich Capital Markets	SEC	44
A.G. Edwards	SEC	44
Hartford	NY*, CT, IL	46
Smith Barney	NYSE, NJ	46
General American Life Insurance	SEC	47
Evergreen Investment	SEC	48
A.B. Watley	N/F	48

Organization	Sanctioning Agency	Months after first case
Rafferty Capital	N/F	50
Ritchie Capital	SEC, NY*	53
Oppenheimer & Co.	N/F	53

N/F = NASD/FINRA, State Attorney Generals are represented by two letter postal code.

*Four NY cases were handled by Andrew Cuomo, after Spitzer was elected Governor.

Appendix 5: Total penalties over time – with regression line

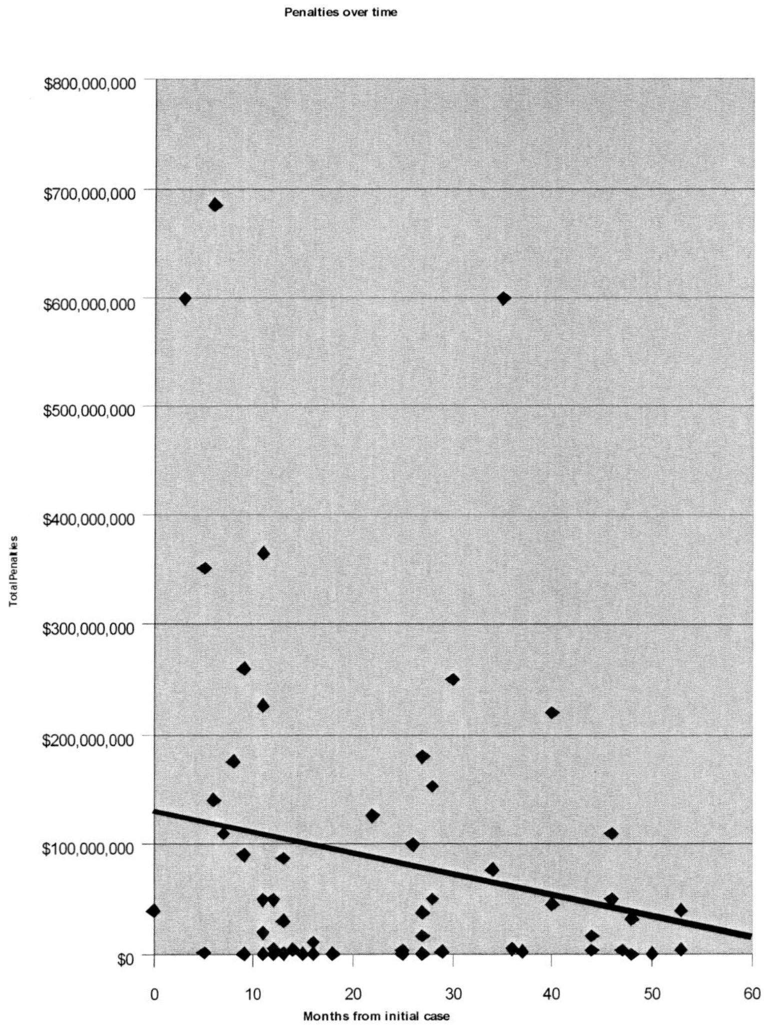

Appendix 6: Penalties over time – Spitzer v. Non-Spitzer penalties with regression lines

Dark Grey = Spitzer cases
Light Grey = Non-Spitzer cases

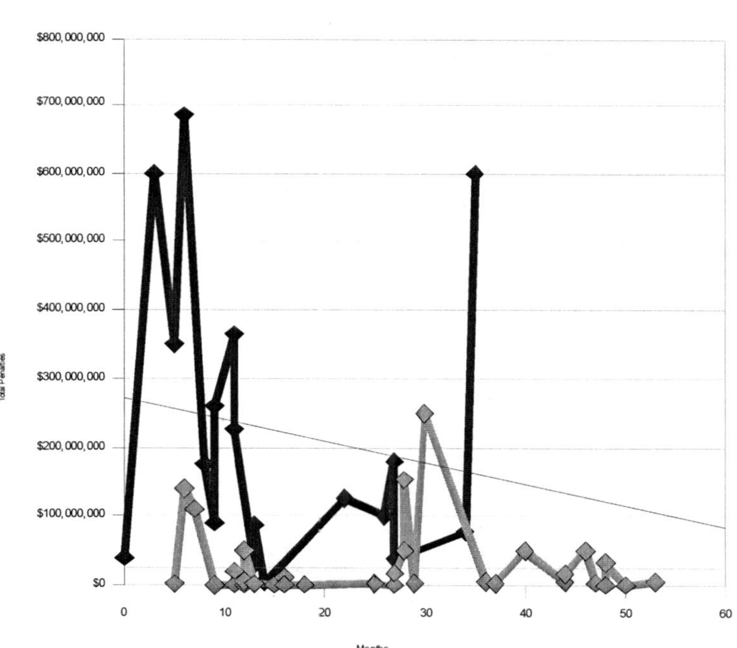

Appendix 7: Total and average penalties*

Type of penalty	Total	Cases	Applicable Mean
Individuals Sanctioned	109	38	2.87
Organizational fine	$1,483,483,000	57	$26,026,018
Disgorgement	$2,669,231,500	51	$52,337,873
Individual Fine	$231,527,000	25	$9,261,080
Fee Reduction	$1,061,000,000	14	$75,785,714.00
Total Penalty	$5,445,241,500	62	$87,826,476

*Mean is calculated using only the cases where that type of penalty was applied.

References

Anderson, J. (2005, November 22). In rarity, Spitzer drops case. *New York Times*. Retrieved from http://www.nytimes.com/.

Atlas, R.D. (2003, September 12). Bank of America executive is said to have departed. *New York Times*. Retrieved from http://www.nytimes.com/.

—. (2003, December 27). He's the other force in the fund investigation. *New York Times*. Retrieved from http://www.nytimes.com/.

—. (2004, May 21). Fund executive accepts life ban in trading case. *New York Times*. Retrieved from http://www.nytimes.com/.

—. (2004, August 26). For mutual funds, first the slap. Now comes the pinch. *New York Times*. Retrieved from http://www.nytimes.com/.

Atlas, R.D., & Abelson, R. (2005, June 10). Ex-broker acquitted in fund case. *New York Times*. Retrieved from http://www.nytimes.com/.

Ayres, I., & Braithwaite, J. (1992). *Responsive Regulation: Transcending the deregulation debate*. New York: Oxford University Press.

Bank of America. (2004). *Portrait of a bank. Annual report.* http://media.corporate-ir.net/media_files/irol/71/71595/reports/2004_ar.pdf.

Becker, H.S. (1963). *Outsiders: Studies in the sociology of deviance*. New York: The Free Press.

Beltran, L. (2004, March 15). Bank of America, Fleet to pay $675 million fine. *CNN Money*. Retrieved from http://money.cnn.com/.

Black, W.K. (2005). *The best way to rob a bank is to own one*. Austin: University of Texas Press.

Blackwell Encyclopedia of Sociology. (2009, May 5). *Moral Entrepreneur*. Retrieved from http://www.sociologyencyclopedia.com/.

Bogle, J.C. (2005). *The battle for the soul of capitalism*. New Haven, CT: Yale University Press.

Boulton, D. (1978). *The grease machine*. New York: Harper & Row.

Braithwaite, J. (January 1993). Transnational regulation of the pharmaceutical industry. *Annals of the American Academy of Political and Social Science, 525*, 12-30.

Brandeis, L. (1913, December 20). Other People's Money, Chapter 5: What publicity can do. *Harper's Weekly*. Retrieved from http://www.law.louisville.edu/library/.

Brown, D. (2003). *Supreme Court of the State of New York Complaint: State of New York, Plaintiff against Capital Canary Partners, LLC, Capital Canary Investment Management, LLC, Capital Canary Partner, LTD and Edward J. Stern, Defendants*. Office of New York State Attorney General Office. Retrieved from http://www.oag.state.ny.us/.

Burns, J. (2003, November 10). SEC chief pledges action on funds; Donaldson mulls measures to eliminate late trading, calls problems 'pervasive'. *Wall Street Journal*. C19.

—. (2004, December 28). Skepticism rings industry cleanup; money managers believe moves to combat abuses will be ineffective, costly. *Wall Street Journal*. C15.

Burton, J. (2003, September 18). Week's top mutual fund stories. *CBS Marketwatch*. Retrieved from http://www.marketwatch.com/.

Calavita, K., & Pontell, H.N. (1994). The state and white-collar crime: Saving the Savings and Loans. *Law and Society Review, 28(2)*, 297-324.

Calavita, K., & Pontell, H.N. (1995). Saving the Savings and Loans? U.S. government response to financial crime. In F. Pearce and L. Snider (Eds.). *Corporate crime: Contemporary debates* (pp. 199-213). Toronto: University of Toronto Press.

Calavita, K.; Pontell, H.N.; & Tillman, R. (1997). *Big money crime*. Berkeley: University of California Press.

CBS News. (2010, April 17). Geithner: Financial Overhaul Bill Will Pass. *CBS News*. Retrieved from http://www.cbsnews.com/

Center for Responsive Politics. (2008, April 16). *Politicians & Elections: Presidential*. Retrieved from www.opensecrets.org/.

Chambliss, W. (1967). Types of deviance and the effectiveness of legal sanctions. *Wisconsin Law Review, 70(3)*, 703-719.

Chambliss, W. (1993). On lawmaking. In W. Chambliss. and M. Zatz (Eds.). *Making law: The state, the law, and structural contradictions* (pp. 3-35). Indiana University Press: Bloomington.

Ciccotello, C.S.; Edelen, R.M.; Greene, J.T.; & Hodges, C.W. (2002). Trading at stale prices with modern technology: Policy options for mutual funds in the internet age. *Virginia Journal of Law and Technology, 3(7)*.

Clinard, M.B. (1983). *Corporate ethics and crime: The role of middle management*. Beverly Hills, CA: Sage.

CNN. (2004, November 17). Pilgrim Baxter guys settle for $160 million. *CNN Money*. Retrieved from http://money.cnn.com/.

Coleman, J. (1987). Toward an integrated theory of white-collar crime. *The American Journal of Sociology, 93(2)*, 406-439.

Conrad, P., & Schneider, J.W. (1992). *Deviance and medicalization*. Philadelphia: Temple University Press.

Cox, C. (2006, September 6). *Testimony concerning options backdating*. U.S. Senate Committee on Banking, Housing, and Urban Affairs.

Cressey, D. (1953). *Other people's money: A study in the social psychology of embezzlement*. New York: Free Press.

Daily Show. (2010, March 8). *Interview with Harry Markopolos*.

Dale, A. (2003, November 26). Firms' late-trading role is probed; NASD broker dealer sweep so far yields 30 referrals to enforcement division. *Wall Street Journal* (Eastern edition). D9.

Dale, A. (2005, January 27). Janus tightens pay-performance tie; compensation plan aims to rebuild investor trust; outflows weigh on profit. *Wall Street Journal*. C17.

Damato, K., & Burns, J. (2004, April 5). Cleaning up the fund industry. *Wall Street Journal*. R1.

Department of Justice. (2004, November 4). *American International Group, Inc. enters into agreements with the United States*. Retrieved from http://judiciary.house.gov/.

Department of Treasury. (2009, June 17). *Financial Regulatory Reform: A new foundation*.

Dugas, C. (2003, November 20). Probe into mutual fund abuse widens. *USA Today*. Retrieved from http://www.usatoday.com/.

—. (2004, February 5). MFS to pay $225 million, executives barred in trading probe. *USA Today*. Retrieved from http://www.usatoday.com/.

—. (2004, February 9). After settlement, MFS hires fund vet Pozen. *USA Today*. Retrieved from http://www.usatoday.com/.

Easterbrook, F.H., & Fischel, D.R. (1991). *The economic structure of corporate laws*. Cambridge, MA: Harvard University Press.

Elkind, P. (2004, April 19). The secrets of Eddie Stern. *Fortune, 8*, 106-128.

Fidelity. (2007, July 15). *Mutual fund basics*. Retrieved from http://scs.fidelity.com/.

Fisse, B., & Braithwaite, J. (1983). *The impact of publicity on corporate offenders*. Albany: State University of New York Press.

—. (1993). *Corporations, crime and accountability*. New York: Cambridge University Press.

Fornelli, C. (2004, November 13). Regulation of Investment Advisers: The view from Washington. Speech by SEC staff. Philadelphia, PA.

Freeman, J.P., & Brown, S.L. (2001). Mutual fund advisory fees: The cost of conflicts of interest. *Journal of Corporation Law, 26(3),* 609–673.

Freidson, E. (1988). *Profession of Medicine: A study of the sociology of applied knowledge.* Chicago: University of Chicago Press.

Fried, C. (2004, January 11). Mutual funds report: Pressure builds to cut fund fees. *New York Times.* Retrieved from http://www.nytimes.com/.

Friedman, M. (1962). *Capitalism and freedom.* Chicago: University of Chicago Press.

GAO (June 2000). *Mutual fund fees: Additional disclosure could encourage price competition.* Report to the Chairman, Subcommittee on Finance and Hazardous Materials; and the Ranking Member, Committee on Commerce, House of Representatives.

—. (May 3, 2001). *SEC's report provides useful information on mutual fund fees and recommends improved fee disclosure.* Letter to John D. Dingell, Ranking Minority Member, Committee on Energy and Commerce, House of Representatives.

—. (May 2002). *Securities markets: Competition and multiple regulators heighten concerns about self-regulation.* Report to Congressional Committees.

—. (April 20, 2004). *SEC operations: Oversight of mutual fund industry presents management challenges.* Testimony before the Subcommittee on Government Efficiency and Financial Management, Committee on Government Reform, House of Representatives.

—. (April 2005). *Mutual fund trading abuses: Lessons can be learned from SEC not having detected violations at an earlier stage.* Report to the Committee on the Judiciary, House of Representatives.

—b. (May 2005). *Mutual fund trading abuses: SEC consistently applied procedures in setting penalties, but could strengthen internal controls.* Report to Congressional Requesters.

—c. (June 7, 2005). *SEC mutual fund oversight: Positive actions are being taken, but regulatory challenges remain.* Testimony before the Subcommittee on Commercial and Administrative Law, Committee on the Judiciary, House of Representatives.

—d. (August 2005). *Mutual fund industry: SEC's revised examination approach offers potential benefits, but significant oversight challenges remain.* Report to Congressional Requesters.

Garfinkel, H. (1956). Conditions of successful degradation ceremonies. *American Journal of Sociology, 61(5),* 420-424.

Gasparino, C. (2005). *Blood on the street*. New York: Free Press.

Geis, G. (1967). The heavy electrical equipment antitrust cases of 1961. In M. Clinard and R. Quinney (Eds.). *Criminal behavior systems* (pp. 139-150). New York: Holt, Rinehart & Winston.

—. (1991). The case study method in sociological criminology. In J.R. Feagin, et al. (Ed.). *A case for the case study* (pp 200-223). Chapel Hill: University of North Carolina Press.

Gilpin, K.N. (2003, November 2). Market Insight: How scandal can help the fund industry. *New York Times*. Retrieved from http://www.nytimes.com/.

Goetz, B. (1997). Organization as class bias in local law enforcement: Arson for profit as a "nonissue". *Law & Society Review, 31(5)*, 557-587.

Goldstein, M. (2003, November 13). Focus in fund scandal turns to Bear Sterns. *The Street*. Retrieved from http://www.thestreet.com/.

—. (2003, December 2). Oppenheimer's Sassano and the market timers. *The Street*. Retrieved from http://www.thestreet.com/.

—. (2005, June 07). Mutual fund jury near verdict. *The Street*. Retrieved from http://www.thestreet.com/.

—. (2005, July 20). How CIBC cashed in on mutual fund fraud. *The Street*. Retrieved from http://www.thestreet.com/.

—. (2005, August 02). Prudential broker criminally charged in fund scandal. *The Street*. Retrieved from http://www.thestreet.com/.

—. (2005, August 30). Defanged Spitzer spares fund crooks jail time. *The Street*. Retrieved from http://www.thestreet.com/.

—. (2006, August 28). Prudential settles for $600 million. *The Street*. Retrieved from http://www.thestreet.com/.

Grabosky, P.; Braithwaite, J.; & Wilson, P. (1987). The myth of community tolerance toward white-collar crime. *Australian and New Zealand Journal of Criminology, 20(1)*, 33-44.

Grace, C. (2009, November 14). The interview. *BBC*. Retrieved from http://www.bbc.co.uk/.

Greenberg, G. (2004, July 22). Trading scandal will divide results of fund scandal. *The Street*. Retrieved from http://www.thestreet.com/.

Gusfield, J. (1955). *Symbolic crusade*. Urbana: University of Illinois Press.

Hagan, J., & Nagel, I. (1982). White-collar crime, white-collar time: The sentencing of white-collar offenders in the South District of New York. *American Criminal Law Review, 20(2)*, 259-289.

Hagan, J.; Nagel, I.; Albonetti, C. (1980). The differential sentencing of white collar offenders in ten federal district courts. *American Sociological Review, 45(5)*, 802-820.

Hagan, J., & Palloni, A. (1986). "Club fed" and the sentencing of white-collar offenders before and after Watergate. *Criminology, 24*, 603-621.

Hakim, D., & Rashbaum, W.K. (2008, March 10). Spitzer, linked to a sex ring as a client, offers apology. *New York Times*. Retrieved from http://www.nytimes.com/.

Hamilton, W. (2003, July 17). Weill retiring in January as chief of Citigroup / Reputation was tarnished by stock-analyst conflict of interest scandal. *San Francisco Gate Chronicle*. Retrieved from http://www.sfgate.com.

Henriques, D.B. (2003, December 11). Fund compliance plans ignored trade timing. *New York Times*. Retrieved from http://www.nytimes.com/

Houge, T., & Wellman, J., (2005). Fallout from the mutual fund trading scandal. *Journal of Business Ethics, 62*, 129–139.

Jenkins, A., & Braithwaite, J. (1993). Profits, pressure and corporate lawbreaking. *Crime, Law, and Social Change, 20(3)*, 221-232.

Jesilow, P.; Pontell, H.N.; & Geis, G. (1993). *Prescription for profit: How doctors defraud Medicaid*. Berkeley: University of California Press.

Johannes, L. (2005, January 24). Strong Performers Suffer Less in Mutual Fund Scandals. *Wall Street Journal*. p. C1.

Kellogg, K. (1977). From retribution to "deserts": The evolution of criminal punishment, *Criminology, 15(2)*, 179-192.

Labaton, S. (2006, April 8). Setback for two rules on mutual funds. *New York Times*. Retrieved from http://www.nytimes.com/.

Lehrer, J. (1996, December 6). The power of Alan Greenspan. *Online News Hour*. Retrieved from http://www.pbs.org/.

Levi, M. (1981). *Phantom capitalists: The organisation and control of long firm fraud*. London: Heineman Educational.

—. (1984). Giving creditors the business: The criminal law in inaction. *International Journal of the Sociology of Law, 12*, 321-333.

Levine, C. (2006, August 22). Get on the omnibus: The mutual fund industry gears up for 22c-2. *Wall Street & Technology*. Retrieved from http://www.wallstreetandtech.com/.

Levitz, J. (2006, February 27). Brand taint, soft returns plague Putnam. *Wall Street Journal*. p. C9.

Lombardi, M. (1999). George Bush, Harken Energy, and Jackson Stephens. c. 1979-90. 5th version.

Lukes, S. (1974). *Power: A radical view*. London: Macmillan.

Lutton, L. P. (2007, March 12). Letter to SEC: Make fund boards more independent. *Morningstar*. Retrieved from http://news.morningstar.com/

Markopolos, H. (2009). *No one would listen: a true financial thriller*. New York: Wiley, John, & Sons.

Maurer, B. (2005). Due diligence and 'reasonable man,' offshore. *Cultural Anthropology, 20(4)*, 474-505.

McCarthy, R. (Ed.). (1959). *Drinking and intoxication*. New Haven, CT and New York: Yale Center of Alcohol Studies and The Free Press of Glencoe.

McCoy, K. (2009, February 12). Pursuer of Madoff blew whistle for nine years. *USA Today*. Retrieved from http://www.usatoday.com/.

McDonald, I. (2005, December 14). More Funds Trim Fees to Restore Trust of Investors. *Wall Street Journal*. C1.

McGeehan, P. (2004, January 11). Mutual funds report; a scandal, but business booms. *New York Times*. Retrieved from http://www.nytimes.com/.

McGrath, W. (2011, June 13). Supreme Court holds that mutual fund investment adviser is not liable for statements made by the mutual fund in the fund's prospectus. Retrieved from http://www.fedseclaw.com.

McLean, B., & Elkind, P. (2003). *The smartest guys in the room*. New York: Penguin Group.

McTamaney, R. (2003). New York's Martin Act: Expanding enforcement in an era of securities regulation. *Washington Legal Foundation, 18(5)*, 1-5.

Meyer, D. (2002, June 26). A few bad apples or a rotten tree? *CBS News*. Retrieved from http://www.cbsnews.com/.

Middlemiss, J. (2010, September 22). Three mutual fund companies look to settle market timing class action. *Financial Post*. Retrieved from http://business.financialpost.com/.

Morgensen, G. (2003, November 16). Market watch: Slapping wrists as the fund scandal spreads. *New York Times*. Retrieved from http://www.nytimes.com/.

Moyer, E. (2005, October 12). Ex-Bank of America broker Sihpol in $220k settlement. *Forbes*. Retrieved from http://www.forbes.com/.

MSNBC. (2003, December 19). Alliance agrees to $600 million settlement. Retrieved from http://www.msnbc.msn.com/.

—. (2004, March 15). Bank of America, FleetBoston agree to settle. Retrieved from http://www.msnbc.msn.com/.

—. (2004, April 27). Janus settles improper-trading case. Retrieved from http://www.msnbc.msn.com/.

—. (2004, August 18). Janus finalizes settlement over improper trades. Retrieved from http://www.msnbc.msn.com/.

NASD/FINRA. (2004, May 12). *NASD's Glauber announces mutual fund task force*. Retrieved from http://www.finra.org/.

—. (2004, May 27). *NASD Names 20 To Mutual Fund Task Force*. Retrieved from http://www.finra.org/.

—. (2006, August 28). *Prudential Securities, Inc. ordered to pay regulators*

$600 million to resolve fraud, other charges relating to improper market timing. Retrieved from http://www.finra.org/.

Needleman M.L., & Needleman, C. (1979). Organizational crime: Two models of criminogenesis. *The Sociological Quarterly, 20(3)*, 517-528.

New York Office of the Attorney General. (2003, October 16). *New York Attorney General and SEC bring criminal and civil actions against mutual fund executive*. Retrieved from http://www.ag.ny.gov/.

—. (2003, November 25). *Former trust officials arrested in late trading fraud*. Retrieved from http://www.ag.ny.gov/.

New York Times Editorial. (2011, June 14). So no one's responsible? Retrieved from http://www.nytimes.com/.

Nocera, J. (2005, July 23). Donaldson: The exit interview. *New York Times*. Retrieved from http://www.nytimes.com/.

O'Connor, James (1973). *The fiscal crisis of the state*. New York: St. Martin's Press.

Offe, C. (1974). Structural problems of the capitalist state: Class rule and the political system: On the selectiveness of political institutions. In K. von Beyrne (Ed.). *German political studies*. Beverly Hills, CA: Sage Publications.

Olver, L. (2008, November 28). CIBC, former trader Flynn settle market timing feud. *Forbes*. Retrieved from http://www.reuters.com/.

Perez-Pena, R. (2000, November 16). Power plants to cut emissions faulted in Northeast smog. *New York Times*. Retrieved from http://www.nytimes.com/.

Pethokoukis, J. (2010, April 16). Analysis: SEC tries to ride Goldman back to credibility. *Reuters*. Retrieved from http://www.reuters.com/.

Potts, G. (1972). *Understanding investments and mutual funds*. New York: Arco Publishing Company.

Pontell, H.N. (1984). *A capacity to punish: The ecology of crime and punishment*. Bloomington: Indiana University Press.

—. (2004). White-collar crime or just risky business? The role of fraud in major financial debacles. *Crime, Law, and Social Change, 42(4-5)*, 309-324.

Pontell, H.N.; Rosoff, S.; & Peterson, A. (2007). Lenient justice? Punishing white-collar and corporate crime. In S. Shoham (Ed.). *The international comparative handbook of penology and criminal justice* (pp. 709-731). Ontario, Canada: de Sitter Publications.

Poulantzas, N. (1969). The problem of the capitalist state. *New Left Review, 58*, 67-78.

Prudential. (2006). *Director's report: Prudential at a glance*. Annual Report. http://www.prudential.co.uk/.

Reiss Jr., A.J. (1984). Selecting strategies of social control over organizational life. In K. Hawkins, & J.M. Thomas (Eds.). *Enforcing regulation* (pp. 23 35). Boston: Kluwer Nijhoff.

Roane, K.R. (2007, April 15). Confounding his critics. *U.S. News & World Report*. Retrieved from http://www.usnews.com/.

Rosen, E. (2006, November 17). Street scene: Savoring a small victory after a market timing scandal. *New York Times*. Retrieved from http://www.nytimes.com/.

Russell, R. (2007). *An introduction to mutual funds worldwide*. Chicester, England: John Wiley & Sons Ltd.

Schwager, J.D. (1992). *The New Market Wizards*. New York: Harper Business.

SEC. (1999, March 22). *SEC Chairman Arthur Levitt proposes significant reforms to mutual fund governance structure*. Retrieved from http://www.sec.gov/.

—. (2002, December 20). *SEC, NY Attorney General, NASD, NASAA, NYSE and state regulators announce historic agreement to reform investment practices; $1.4 billion global settlement includes penalties and funds for investors*. Retrieved from http://www.sec.gov/.

—. (2003, October 16). *New York AG and SEC bring criminal and civil actions against mutual fund executive*. Retrieved from http://www.sec.gov/.

—. (2003, November 13). *Putnam agrees to make restitution and implement immediate, significant structural reforms in partial resolution of SEC enforcement action*. Retrieved from http://www.sec.gov/.

—. (2003, November 19). *SEC adopts rules on disclosure of nominating committee functions and communications between security holders and boards of directors*. Retrieved from http://www.sec.gov/.

—. (2003, November 25). *SEC charges Security Trust Company, N.A. And three former executives for facilitating fraudulent mutual fund late trading and market timing schemes*. Retrieved from http://www.sec.gov/.

—. (2003, December 18). *Alliance Capital Management will pay record $250 million and make significant governance and compliance reforms to settle SEC charges*. Retrieved from http://www.sec.gov/.

—. (2004, February 5). *Massachusetts Financial Services Co. will pay $225 million and make significant governance and compliance reforms to settle SEC fraud charges concerning mutual fund market timing*. Retrieved from http://www.sec.gov/.

—. (2004, April 1). *Security Trust Company, N.A. pays $1 million in mutual fund market timing and late trading fraud action*. Retrieved from http://www.sec.gov/.

—. (2004, April 8). *Putnam agrees to pay $55 million to resolve SEC enforcement action related to market timing by portfolio managers*.

Retrieved from http://www.sec.gov/.

—. (2004, September 30). *Investment Company Act of 1940*. Retrieved from http://www.sec.gov/about/laws/ica40.pdf.

—. (2004, November 17). *Harold Baxter and Gary Pilgrim agree to pay a total of $160 million to settle fraud charges concerning undisclosed market timing*. Retrieved from http://www.sec.gov/.

—. (2008, May 29). *SEC promotes long-time enforcement attorney Marc Fagel to director of San Francisco region*. Retrieved from http://www.sec.gov/.

—. (2009, September 4). *Investigation of the failure of the SEC to uncover Bernard Madoff's Ponzi scheme* (public version). Retrieved from http://www.sec.gov/.

—. (2011, July 18). *Court enters order against former prudential registered representatives in connection with deceptive market timing practices*. Retrieved from http://www.sec.gov/.

—. (2011, December 16). *Jury Finds Former Prudential Securities Registered Representative Liable For Deceptive Mutual Fund Market Timing Practices*. Retrieved from http://www.sec.gov/.

Sender, H., & Zuckerman, M. (2003, December 9). Behind the mutual fund probe: 3 informants open up. *Wall Street Journal*. C1.

Sender, H., et. al. (2003, December 9). More traders drawn into mutual-fund probe; Goodwin, formerly at Canary, tells investigators of 'late trades'; many hedge funds subpoenaed. *Wall Street Journal* (Eastern edition). C1.

Shapiro, S. (1985). The road not taken: The elusive path to criminal prosecution
for white-collar offenders. *Law and Society Review, 19*, 179-217.

—. (1990). Collaring the crime, not the criminal: Reconsidering the concept of white-collar crime. *American Sociological Review, 55(June)*, 346-365.

Shinal, J. (2003, November 18). Mutual fund scandal: CalPERS fires manager. *San Francisco Gate*. Retrieved from http://www.sfgate.com/.

Simanauskas, L., & Kucko, I. (2004). Trends of the investment fund industry development. *Ekonomika, 66*, 1-22.

Simpson, S. (2002). *Corporate crime, law, and social control*. Cambridge, UK: Cambridge University Press.

Simpson, S., & Piquero, N. (2002). Low self-control, organizational theory, and corporate crime. *Law & Society Review, 36(3)*, 509-547.

Singer, R.G. (1979). *Just deserts: sentencing based on equality and desert*. Cambridge, MA: Ballinger Publishing Company.

Sloan, A. (2003, December 8). The mutual fund scandal: unfair fight. *Newsweek*. Retrieved from http://www.newsweek.com/.

Smith, E.B. (2003, October 30). Strong founder may bow out amid scandal.

USA Today. Retrieved from http://www.usatoday.com/.

Solman, P. (2003, November 26). Newsmaker: William Donaldson. *PBS*. Retrieved from http://www.pbs.org/.

Solomon, D., & Hechinger, J. (2004, June 22). Mutual funds' chiefs might lose strings. *Wall Street Journal*. C1.

Spitzer, E. (2004, January 6). *Statement by Attorney General Eliot Spitzer regarding the Investment Company Institute's mutual fund fee report.* Retrieved from http://www.ag.ny.gov/.

—. (2008, November 16). How to ground the Street; The former 'enforcer' on the best way to keep financial markets in check. *Washington Post*. Retrieved from http://www.washingtonpost.com/.

—. (2010, March 16). Seize power, shareholders. *Slate*. Retrieved from http://www.slate.com/.

Stempel, J. (2008, June 11). NYSE bars 3 ex-Merrill brokers over market timing. *Reuters*. Retrieved from http://www.reuters.com/.

Sutherland, E. (1940). White-collar criminality. *American Sociological Review, 5(1)*, 1-12.

Swensen, D.F. (2005). *Unconventional success: A fundamental approach to personal investment*. New York: Free Press.

Thomas Jr., L. (2004, March 16). Mutual fund tells Wall Street it wants a la carte commissions. *New York Times*. Retrieved from http://www.nytimes.com/.

—. (2005, December 16). Bear Sterns agrees to pay $250 million in fund case. *New York Times*. Retrieved from http://www.nytimes.com/.

—. (2006, August 29). Prudential to pay fine in trading. *New York Times*. Retrieved from http://www.nytimes.com/.

USA Today. (2002, March 24). Enron scandal brings overdue scrutiny of analysts. Retrieved from http://www.usatoday.com/.

—. (2006, August 2). SEC accuses three ex-Janus executives of allowing market timing trades. Retrieved from http://www.usatoday.com/.

USSC. (May 3, 2011). *FY 2010 sourcebook*. Retrieved from http://www.ussc.gov/.

Valdmanis, T. (October 2, 2006). Senate report blasts SEC's Enron oversight. *USA Today*. Retrieved from http://www.usatoday.com/.

van den Haag, E. (1975). *Punishing criminals: Concerning a very old and painful question*. New York: Basic Books.

Vaughan, D. (1983). *Controlling unlawful corporate behavior: Social structure and corporate misconduct*. Chicago: University of Chicago Press.

Vicini, J. (2010, March 30). Supreme Court hands victory to mutual fund industry. Reuters. Retrieved from http://reuters.com/.

von Hirsch, A. (1976). *Doing Justice: The choice of punishments*. New York: Hill and Wang.

Waldman, D.E. (1978). *Antitrust action and market structure*. Lexington, MA: Lexington Books.

Wall Street Journal (1999). *Guide to Understanding Money & Investing*. New York: Lightbulb Press.

Weber, J. (2004, September 6). Putting a new face on Janus. *BusinessWeek*. Retrieved from http://www.businesweek.com/.

Weisburd, D.; Waring, E.; & Wheeler, S. (1990). Class, status, and the punishment of white-collar criminals. *Law and Social Inquiry, 15*, 223-239

Weiss, G. (2006, March 25). A fine that fits the crime. *New York Times*. Retrieved from http://www.nytimes.com/.

Wheeler, S. (1992). The problem of white-collar crime motivation. In K. Schlegel & D. Weisburd (Eds.). *White-collar crime reconsidered* (pp. 108 123). Boston: Northeastern University Press.

Wheeler, S., & Rothman, M.L. (1982). The organization as weapon in white collar crime. *Michigan Law Review, 80(7)*, 1403-1426.

Yost, P. (2005, June 21). Court clouds future of mutual fund rules. *USA Today*. Retrieved from http://www.usatoday.com/.

Zitzewitz, E. (2003). Who cares about shareholders? Arbitrage-proofing mutual funds. *Journal of Law, Economics, and Organization, 19(2)*, 245-280.

—. (2006). How widespread was late trading in funds? *American Economic Review (Papers & Proceedings)*, 284-289.

Zweig, J. (2009, August 15). Can the Supreme Court undress high fund fees? *Wall Street Journal*. Retrieved from http://online.wsj.com/.

Index

T